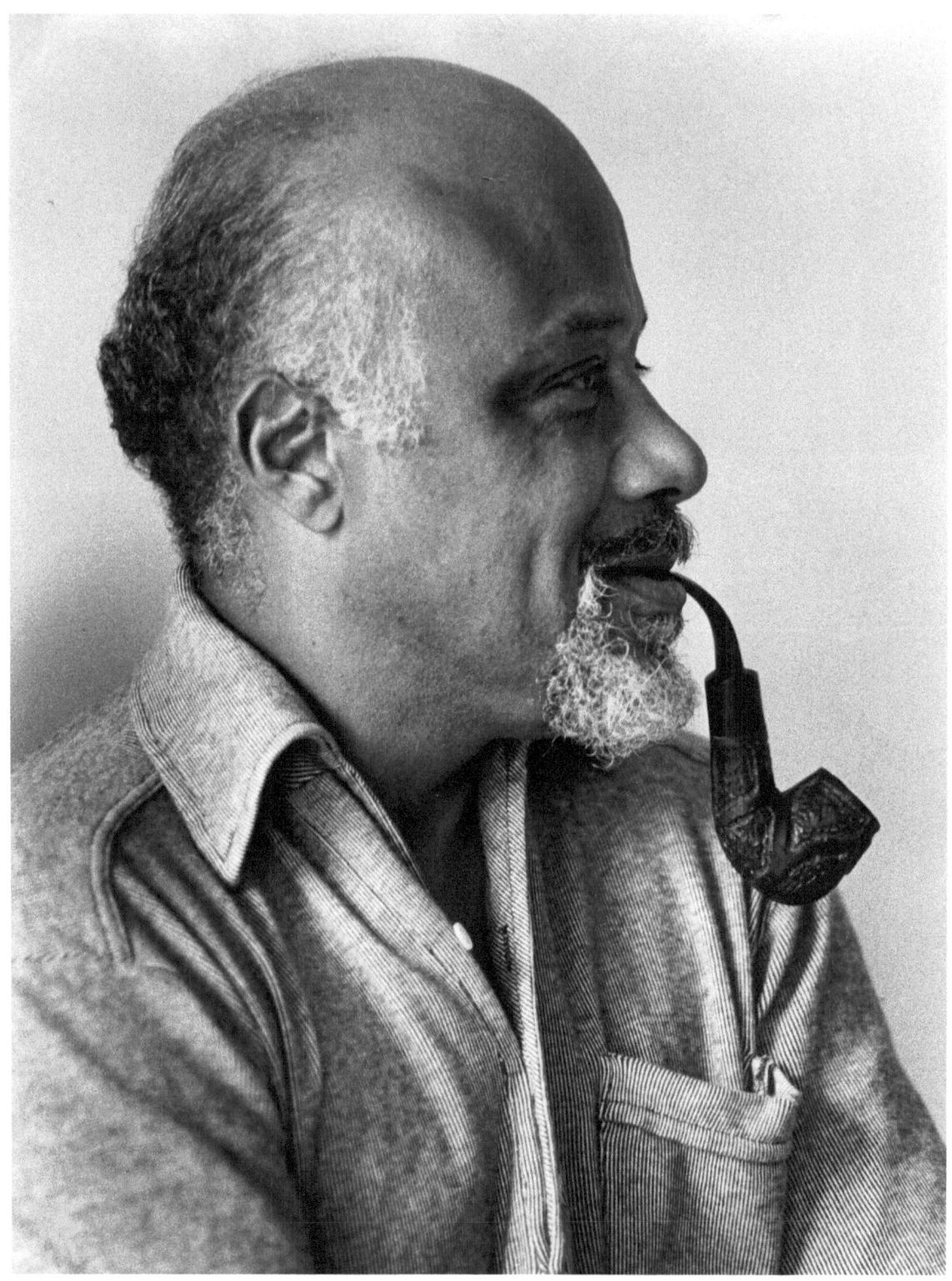

Fig. 1, Paul F. Keene, Jr. (1920-2009), 1984, Photograph. Courtesy of the Keene family.

Paul Keene:
Post-War Explorations in Painting

Edited by
Klare Scarborough

ISBN-10: 0-9983283-0-8

ISBN-13: 978-0-9983283-0-0

Paul Keene: Post-War Explorations in Painting

Contributors: Bianca Desamour, Paul F. Keene, Jr., Ron Rumford, Klare Scarborough

Design Credit: Josh Ash

Photography Credits:
Photography of Artwork by Paul Keene provided by La Salle University Art Museum, Dolan/Maxwell, the Pennsylvania Academy of the Fine Arts, and Woodmere Art Museum. Historical Photographs provided by Laura Keene.

Artwork by Paul F. Keene, Jr. © 2017 Estate of Paul F. Keene, Jr.

This book has been published with support from The Philadelphia Cultural Fund and La Salle University Art Museum's Art Angels.

Book produced in conjunction with the exhibition:

Paul Keene: Post-War Explorations in Painting, September 28 - December 2, 2016.

ISBN-10: 0-9983283-0-8

ISBN-13: 978-0-9983283-0-0

Printed by Lulu

Cover Image: Paul F. Keene, Jr. (1920-2009), *The Sorceress*, 1956, Oil on Canvas, 23 1/4 x 15 1/4 in., Collection of La Salle University Art Museum, Gift of Benjamin D. Bernstein, 91-P-377.

Back Cover image: Paul F. Keene, Jr. (1920-2009), *Haitian Voodoo Spirits*, 1953, Oil on Wood Panels, 69 1/4 x 80 in. (total), Collection of La Salle University Art Museum, Gift of Benjamin D. Bernstein, 01-P-474(1-3).

Introduction

Paul Keene: Post-War Explorations in Painting showcases the work of Philadelphia-based African American artist Paul Farwell Keene, Jr. (1920-2009), created during the years immediately following World War II. From 1949 to 1951, with support from the G.I. Bill, Keene lived in Paris, France, and from 1952 to 1954, with support from the John Hay Whitney Foundation, he lived in Port-au-Prince, Haiti. The paintings created during his time abroad and through the late 1950s, which are featured in this exhibition, reflect the influence of European Modernism, African art, and an emerging Afro-Caribbean aesthetic.

The catalogue opens with my essay, "Paul Keene in Paris and Haiti," which provides background about the artist and his work, particularly during the post-war years. I focus on Keene's travels and his time living abroad in Paris and Haiti, and the impact of those international experiences on his artistic development. I argue that his professional studies abroad in Paris and particularly in Haiti nurtured his interest in spiritual and mythological themes, and fueled his experimentation with figurative abstraction during the 1950s and beyond.

Following this is an essay by La Salle University graduate, Bianca Desamour (Class of 2016), who completed a curatorial internship at La Salle University Art Museum in spring 2016. Her interest in writing a research paper about Keene stemmed from her experiences traveling to Haiti with La Salle University service trips, and also from her personal connections with family members who had lived in Haiti. Her essay, "Paul Keene and the Haitian Experience," examines the artist's relationship with Haitian artists as well as with Afro-Modernity and the Caribbean avant-garde.

Paul Keene himself also wrote about Haitian artists in a short essay entitled "Haitian Painters," which was published in 1954 in the *Artists Equity Association Newletter, Philadelphia Chapter*. Here, he articulated a strong interest in "the Haitian psychic insight" which was based in the artist's recognition of "Le Mystère." This essay illustrates Keene's views on the convergence of religion and art in Haitian painting.

In the closing essay, Ron Rumford provides some background about the exhibition, and also about plans to travel many of the paintings to other university museums. He tells about the exciting discovery of artworks in the Keene family attic, and the opportunity this presented to learn more about a little-known period in the artist's career. Rumford offers a personal perspective as Keene's gallery representative, fellow artist and friend for many years. He also discusses Keene's associations with other artists, with regard to his artistic training, his teaching, and his network of collegial relationships.

Many people have noted that Keene's successful professional career as an artist and educator helped to raise the visibility of African American artists. He became a model for many young artists, and his paintings continue to inspire and excite audiences today. As he developed as an artist, he was molded by his social and religious upbringing in North Philadelphia, but he was also shaped by his experiences and perspectives gained while living abroad after World War II. This exhibition catalogue provides background and insights on the impact of these travel opportunities on Keene's artistic development and professional success.

Klare Scarborough, Ph.D.
Director and Chief Curator,
La Salle University Art Museum

Acknowledgements

I am first of all grateful to Ron Rumford for suggesting an exhibition about Paul Keene's Haitian works, and also to Laura Keene for providing me with access to information and documentation about her late husband's work. My gratitude extends to Laura and Paul's children, Jacques Keene and Lydia Keene Williams, for their support of the project; and to their close circle of friends, including Anne Kaplan and also Lewis Tanner Moore, who has been wonderfully supportive and a tremendous resource for Keene's work.

I also thank the individuals and institutions that have kindly assisted us with artwork loans and photographs for the exhibition, including Laura Keene; Lewis Tanner Moore; William A. Dodd; Gladys Meyers; Ron Rumford, Jonathan Eckel, Margo Dolan and Peter Maxwell at Dolan/Maxwell; Patricia Wilson Aden and Brittany Webb at the African American Museum in Philadelphia; Jennifer Johns at the Pennsylvania Academy of the Fine Arts; Annetta Stowman at Villanova University; and Rachel McCay and Sally Larson at Woodmere Art Museum.

With regard to programming, I am grateful to Dr. Terry Rey, Associate Professor of Religion at Temple University, for presenting a public lecture on Haitian Voodoo in conjunction with the exhibition. His insights on Haitian culture and religion have enriched our understanding of Keene's experiences in Haiti during the early 1950s.

My acknowledgements extend to Art Museum staff members: Miranda Clark-Binder, Curator of Education and Public Programs, for organizing programs and interpreting the exhibition for visitors; and Rebecca Oviedo, Collections Manager/Registrar, for coordinating preparations for the exhibition, including managing the loan agreements, image permissions, artwork transportation, and installation of text panels and labels. Both of these staff members were involved with copyediting the exhibition and catalogue text. I also want to thank our Curatorial Intern Bianca Desamour for her work on the exhibition and the catalogue.

Special thanks go to Rebecca Oviedo and Jonathan Donovan for photographing artwork and editing digital images; Josh Ash for designing the exhibition catalogue; and La Salle student worker Sarah Mooney for assiting with the design layout. I am also grateful to Mark Wallison for installing the exhibition.

Supporters of the Art Museum's exhibitions and related programs include the Philadelphia Cultural Fund; the Pennsylvania Council on the Arts; the Brother Daniel Burke Endowment Fund; the Art Angels; La Salle University's Departments of Fine Arts, Religion, History, and English; the Multicultural and International Center; the Greater Philadelphia Initiative; the Explorer Connection; and the Concert and Lecture Series. I am also appreciative of ongoing support received from the Office of the Provost and the Office of Mission.

Contents

Catalogue Illustrations

Cat. 1, Paul F. Keene, Jr. (1920-2009), *Pietà, Soisy*, 1951, Oil on Board, 20 x 16 in., Courtesy of the Keene Family and Dolan/Maxwell. Artwork © 2017 Estate of Paul F. Keene, Jr.

Cat. 2, Paul F. Keene, Jr. (1920-2009), *Mother and Son*, 1951, Oil on Canvas, 32 x 21 in., Private Collection. Artwork © 2017 Estate of Paul F. Keene, Jr.

Cat. 3, Paul F. Keene, Jr. (1920-2009), *Symphony in Blue*, 1951, Oil on Canvas, 29 ½ x 25 in., Artwork from Villanova University Collection, Gift of Benjamin D. Bernstein. Artwork © 2017 Estate of Paul F. Keene, Jr.

Cat. 4, Paul F. Keene, Jr. (1920-2009), *Untitled Abstract*, 1951, Graphite and Pastel, 14 x 16 in., Collection of Lewis Tanner Moore. Artwork © 2017 Estate of Paul F. Keene, Jr.

Cat. 5, Paul F. Keene, Jr. (1920-2009), *Abstract*, 1951, Oil on Paper, 22 x 30 in., Artwork from Villanova University Collection, Gift of Edward I. Bernstein. Artwork © 2017 Estate of Paul F. Keene, Jr.

Cat. 6, Paul F. Keene, Jr. (1920-2009), *Soisy-sous-Montmorency*, 1951, Oil on Canvas, 23 x 32 in., Collection of Lewis Tanner Moore. Artwork © 2017 Estate of Paul F. Keene, Jr.

Cat. 7, Paul F. Keene, Jr. (1920-2009), *Untitled (Abstract)*, 1952, Acrylic on Rice Paper, adhered to board, 19 ¼ x 25 in., Courtesy of the Pennsylvania Academy of the Fine Arts, Philadelphia. Gift of Benjamin D. Bernstein and Robin J. Bernstein, 2002.9.13. Artwork © 2017 Estate of Paul F. Keene, Jr.

Cat. 8, Paul F. Keene, Jr. (1920-2009), *Chicken Woman*, 1953, Encaustic on Cardboard, 21 ¼ x 11 in., Courtesy of the Pennsylvania Academy of the Fine Arts, Philadelphia. Gift of Benjamin D. Bernstein, 1959.10.2. Artwork © 2017 Estate of Paul F. Keene, Jr.

Cat. 9, Paul F. Keene, Jr. (1920-2009), *Chicken Woman and Child*, c. 1953, Oil on Canvas, 21 ⅛ x 12 ½ in., Courtesy of Gladys Meyers and Dolan/Maxwell. Artwork © 2017 Estate of Paul F. Keene, Jr.

Cat. 10, Paul F. Keene, Jr. (1920-2009), *Blue Man (Carrying a Coffin)*, c. 1953, Oil on Masonite, 29 x 21 ½ in, Courtesy of Dr. William Dodd and Dolan/Maxwell. Artwork © 2017 Estate of Paul F. Keene, Jr.

Cat. 11, Paul F. Keene, Jr. (1920-2009), *Drummer*, 1952, Oil on Masonite, 48 x 20 in., Artwork from Villanova University Collection, Gift of Benjamin D. Bernstein. Artwork © 2017 Estate of Paul F. Keene, Jr.

Cat. 12, Paul F. Keene, Jr. (1920-2009), *Voodoo Priest*, c. 1953, Oil on Board, 23 ½ x 17 ¾ in., Woodmere Art Museum: Gift from the collection of Benjamin D. Bernstein, 1995. Photography: Rick Echelmeyer. Artwork © 2017 Estate of Paul F. Keene, Jr.

Cat. 13, Paul F. Keene, Jr. (1920-2009), *Arms Up*, c. 1952, Oil on Board, 5 ¾ x 4 in., Courtesy of Dr. William Dodd and Dolan/Maxwell. Artwork © 2017 Estate of Paul F. Keene, Jr.

Cat. 14, Paul F. Keene, Jr. (1920-2009), *Untitled (Haitian)*, c. 1952, Oil on Panel, 15 ⅞ x 12 in, Private Collection, Courtesy of Dolan/Maxwell. Artwork © 2017 Estate of Paul F. Keene, Jr.

Cat. 15, Paul F. Keene, Jr. (1920-2009), *Figure, Haiti*, c. 1952, Oil on Board, 25 ⅝ x 21 ¼ in., Courtesy of the Keene Family and Dolan/Maxwell. Artwork © 2017 Estate of Paul F. Keene, Jr.

Cat. 16, Paul F. Keene, Jr. (1920-2009), *The Sorceress*, 1956, Oil on Canvas, 23 ¼ x 15 ¼ in., Collection of La Salle University Art Museum, Gift of Benjamin D. Bernstein, 91-P-377. Artwork © 2017 Estate of Paul F. Keene, Jr. and La Salle University Art Museum.

Cat. 17, Paul F. Keene, Jr. (1920-2009), *Clarinet Player*, c. 1955, Oil on Masonite, 41 ½ x 24 ½ in., Courtesy of the African American Museum in Philadelphia. Artwork © 2017 Estate of Paul F. Keene, Jr.

Cat. 18, Paul F. Keene, Jr. (1920-2009), *Horseman of the Apocalypse*, 1956, Oil on Artist Board, 30 x 22 in., Collection of Lewis Tanner Moore. Artwork © 2017 Estate of Paul F. Keene, Jr.

Cat. 19, Paul F. Keene, Jr. (1920-2009), *Haiti Abstraction*, c. 1958, Oil on Canvas, 30 ½ x 24 in., Courtesy of the Keene Family and Dolan/Maxwell. Artwork © 2017 Estate of Paul F. Keene, Jr.

Cat. 20, Paul F. Keene, Jr. (1920-2009), *Mardi Gras Parade*, c. 1953, Oil on Canvas, 34 x 52 in., Courtesy of the Keene Family and Dolan/Maxwell. Artwork © 2017 Estate of Paul F. Keene, Jr.

Cat. 21, Paul F. Keene, Jr. (1920-2009), *The Altered Ego*, c. 1955, Oil on Canvas, 53 x 37 ½ in., Courtesy of the Keene Family and Dolan/Maxwell. Artwork © 2017 Estate of Paul F. Keene, Jr.

Cat. 22, Paul F. Keene, Jr. (1920-2009), *Baroque Warriors*, 1957, Oil on Canvas, 59 x 37 ½ in., Courtesy of the Keene Family and Dolan/Maxwell. Artwork © 2017 Estate of Paul F. Keene, Jr.

Cat. 23, Paul F. Keene, Jr. (1920-2009), *Haitian Voodoo Spirits*, 1953, Oil on Wood Panels, 69 ¼ x 80 in. (total), Collection of La Salle University Art Museum, Gift of Benjamin D. Bernstein, 01-P-474(1-3). Artwork © 2017 Paul F. Keene, Jr. and La Salle University Art Museum.

Figure Illustrations

Fig. 1, Paul F. Keene, Jr. (1920-2009), 1984, Photograph. Courtesy of the Keene family.

Fig. 2, Paul F. Keene, Jr. (1920-2009), *Street Musician (Joe's Bar)*, 1947, Oil on Panel, 23 x 18 in., Collection of Lewis Tanner Moore. Artwork © 2017 Estate of Paul F. Keene, Jr.

Fig. 3, Paul F. Keene, Jr. while studying at the Académie Julian, Paris, 1950, Photograph. Courtesy of the Keene family.

Fig. 4, Paul F. Keene, Jr. with colleagues at Galerie Huit, Paris, 1950, Photograph. Courtesy of the Keene family.

Fig. 5, Paul F. Keene, Jr. at the Centre d'Art, Port-au-Prince, Haiti, 1953, Photograph. Courtesy of the Keene family.

Fig. 6, Cover of Exhibition Program by Paul Keene, Jr. (left) and Antonio Joseph (right), Centre d'Art, Port-au-Prince, Haiti, 1953, Relief print on pellum, 6 ¾ x 9 ½ in. Courtesy of the Keene Family and Dolan/Maxwell. Artwork © 2017 Estate of Paul F. Keene, Jr. and Antonio Joseph.

Fig. 7, Paul F. Keene, Jr. (1920-2009), *Haitian Studies*, Ink on Paper, 8 ¾ x 11 ⅞ in., c. 1952. Verso: *Houses at Port-au-Prince*. Courtesy of the Keene Family and Dolan/Maxwell. Artwork © 2017 Estate of Paul F. Keene, Jr.

Fig. 8, Paul F. Keene, Jr. (1920-2009), *Haitian Voodoo Spirits* (Detail of Central Panel), 1953, Oil on Wood Panels, 69 ¼ x 80 in. (total), Collection of La Salle University Art Museum, Gift of Benjamin D. Bernstein, 01-P-474(1-3). Artwork © 2017 Estate of Paul F. Keene, Jr. and La Salle University Art Museum.

Fig. 9, Paul F. Keene, Jr. (1920-2009), Preliminary Sketch for *Horseman of the Apocalypse*, 1950, 10 ¾ x 12 ¾ in., Courtesy of the Keene Family and Dolan/Maxwell. Artwork © 2017 Estate of Paul F. Keene, Jr.

Fig. 10, George Liautaud (1899-1991), *Cross*, c. 1953, Iron. Collection of Laura Keene. © 2017 Estate of George Liautaud.

Fig. 11, George Liautaud (1899-1991) and Paul F. Keene, Jr. (1920-2009), *Haitian Figure*, c. 1953, Iron, Collection of Laura Keene. Artwork © 2017 Estate of George Liautaud and Paul F. Keene, Jr.

Fig. 12, Préfète Duffaut (1923-2012), *Ville Imaginaire*, 1952, Oil on Board, Collection of Laura Keene. Artwork © 2017 Estate of Préfète Duffaut.

Fig. 13, Paul F. Keene, Jr. (1920-2009), *Houses, Port au Prince*, 1952, Watercolor on Paper, 10 x 14 ⅛ in., Private Collection, Courtesy of Dolan/Maxwell. Artwork © 2017 Paul F. Keene, Jr.

Paul Keene in Paris and Haiti

After serving in the United States (U.S.) Army in World War II, Philadelphia-based African American artist Paul Farwell Keene Jr. (1920-2009) took the opportunity to study abroad, living in Paris, France, from 1949 to 1951, and in Port-au-Prince, Haiti, from 1952 to 1954. His sojourn in Paris exposed him directly to European Modernism, particularly Cubism, and to the influence of African art. He experimented with a Cubist splintering of form and with religious subjects such the Crucifixion and Pietà. Subsequently, during his time in Port-au-Prince, Keene became involved with Haitian artists as an instructor at the Centre d'art (Art Center) and became interested in an emerging Afro-Caribbean Modernism. Self-described as an "abstract figurative painter," he began to incorporate bright vibrant colors and to explore formal abstractions, pushing the limits of his figurative representations and layering his paintings with symbolic references and motifs. Some of his paintings include Voodoo religious imagery and reflect his research into the African roots of Haitian artistic and musical traditions.

This curatorial essay focuses on Keene's explorations in painting during the post-war years. After presenting some background about the artist's early life and education, I focus on his travels to Paris and Haiti to examine how Keene's international and transcultural experiences played a formative role in his artistic development. I propose that Keene's paintings during the late 1940s and early 1950s opened the way for his more fluid abstractions of the late 1950s and beyond, and heralded the increasing importance of myth in his work. I argue that Keene's alternation between figuration and abstraction, and his efforts to combine the two forms of artistic expression, reflected his dual engagement with both African American social issues and painterly aesthetics.

Curlee Raven Holton, in his catalogue essay for the Michener Art Museum retrospective, *Paul Keene: His Art and His Legacy* (2005), provides a wealth of biographical information which is summarized only briefly here.[1] Born in 1920, Keene grew up in a middle class family in North Philadelphia. Both of his parents were undertakers, and the family lived above the funeral parlor business at 16th and Thompson Streets, near the campus of Temple University. He attended the nearby Central High School, the training ground of many great Philadelphia artists, graduating in 1938.[2] He initially wanted to become a commercial illustrator, so he enrolled at the Philadelphia Museum and School of Industrial Art (now University of the Arts), earning a diploma in Illustration in June 1942.[3] When World War II broke out, Keene enlisted in the U.S. Army Air Corps, attaining the rank of lieutenant. He became a Navigator with the Tuskegee Airmen in the 332nd Fighter Group.[4] After the war ended, with support from the G.I. Bill, Keene earned two college degrees as well as a Masters of Fine Arts from Temple University's Tyler School of Art in 1948.[5]

While he was still a student, Keene also began exhibiting artwork at local institutions such as the Dubin Gallery and also the Pyramid Club, located at 1517 West Girard Avenue. The Pyramid Club was established in 1937 as a center for social, intellectual and artistic activity among black professionals. From 1941 to the late 1950s, the Club hosted annual invitational art exhibitions and became known for its progressive interracial art shows.[6] Scholars have noted the prevailing dialogue between heritage and craft at the time, with noted scholar Alain Locke emphasizing the importance of African heritage and black subjects, and influential educators like Allan Freelon stressing the craft and freedom of painting—a dialogue that shaped Keene's work and that of generations of African American artists to come.[7] We can see this in Keene's preference for subject matter rooted in African American experience, and in his love for artistic materials and techniques of painting, for colors, textures, and abstractions.

Many of Keene's early paintings emerged from a Social Realist and American Scene tradition, with imagery drawn from African American urban life and culture.[8] As he later recalled in an interview for the Archives of American Art, his work from the 1940s was "[m]ostly figurative, involved with being black, I guess. Just the things I knew—musicians, clubs, streets of North Philadelphia."[9] Among his favorite subjects were black street performers, including clowns and musicians. Works such as *Street Musician (Joe's Bar)* (1947) [fig. 2],

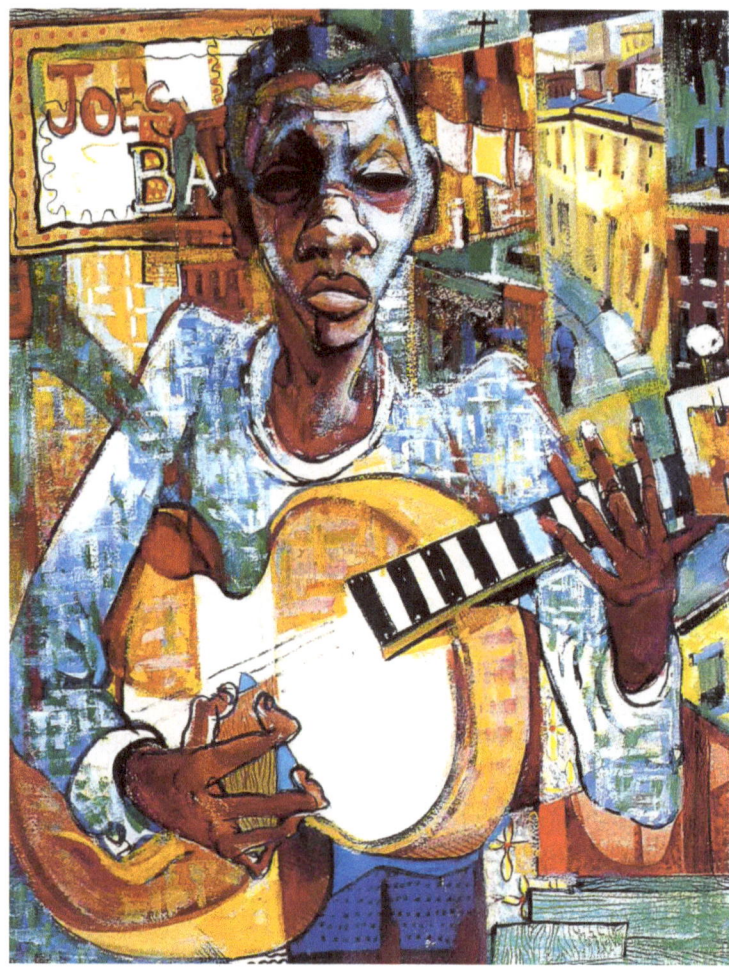

Fig. 2, Paul F. Keene, Jr. (1920-2009), *Street Musician (Joe's Bar)*, 1947, Oil on Panel, 23 x 18 in., Collection of Lewis Tanner Moore. Artwork © 2017 Estate of Paul F. Keene, Jr.

illustrate Keene's early interest in figural representation and urban subject matter, as well as his tendencies toward abstraction, particularly in his juxtaposition of background elements to create the effect of a palimpsest or collage—an effect that Keene would explore in many later works.

Keene's depictions of black street performers emerged from his ongoing interest in African American musical traditions, particularly jazz. He claimed that he knew all of the musicians who lived in his North Philadelphia neighborhood, noting that Philadelphia was "a good jazz town," "the stopping place before you made the big time in New York."[10] He remarked that he would visit jazz clubs and watch jazz musicians very closely as they played, then he would return to his studio and make sketches based on his memories.[11] Keene also perceived close associations between jazz music and religious music, and he noted that

some of his paintings of street musicians "had to do with the black storefront church." He explained, "They were all over the place—every other block there was a church. And I used to go just because the music was so great. We used to stand outside and listen to them."[12]

During the late 1940s, alongside his interest in figural representation, Keene also explored more abstract and symbolic means of rendering form, particularly with his paintings of landscapes. His painting entitled *What a Tale These Bones Could Tell*, exhibited at the Pyramid Club annual in 1948, prompted one reviewer to compare him with American Symbolist painter Albert Pinkman Ryder.[13] Keene later noted that he was working in both figurative and abstract modes at the time, and that he would "oscillate between the two," recalling that even then he was seeking "a position that allowed the two of them to sit together."[14] It is interesting to consider

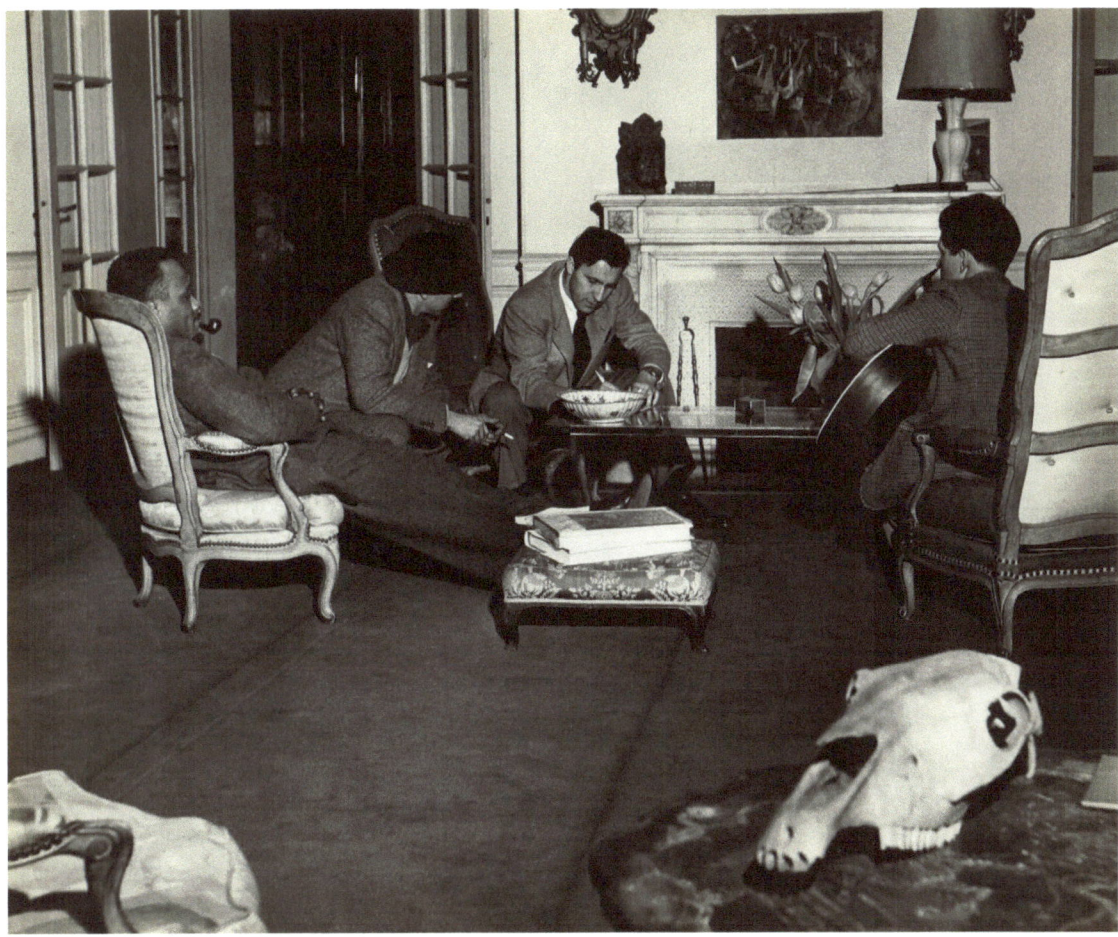

Fig. 3, Paul F. Keene, Jr. while studying at the Académie Julian, Paris, 1950, Photograph. Courtesy of the Keene family.

Keene's early experiments in abstraction, as well as his interest in spirituality, mysticism and myth, in relation to post-war Modernist currents, particularly Cubism and Non-Objective art in Europe, and Abstract Expressionism which dominated the New York City art scene in the 1940s and 1950s.[15] Keene was well aware of these artistic movements, and he frequently travelled up and down the East Coast of the U.S. to view museums and exhibitions.[16]

In 1949, Keene took the opportunity to study abroad in Paris, France. He later noted that he had always wanted to go to Paris, but his move was precipitated when he was denied a teaching position at Penn State University because of his race.[17] He later related that the horrible interview experience spurred his anger and solidified his decision to leave the U.S. Thus, with his new wife, Laura Mitchell, Keene used his final two years of G.I. Bill funding to live in Paris and study at the Académie

Julian from 1949 to 1951.[18] During his time in Paris, he was directly exposed to Cubism and other forms of Non-Objective and Modernist art. He also became more aware of the impact of African art in contemporary abstract expression.

Soon after arriving in Paris, Keene connected with Tyler alumni such as Robert (Bob) Rosenwald, the nephew of the famous art collector Lessing Rosenwald; and he became involved with the opening of Rosenwald's Galerie Huit, which provided an exhibition space for American artists in Paris.[19] He connected with other American artists living abroad, such as Haywood (Bill) Rivers, Romare Bearden, and Sam Francis, and with the British artist Stanley William Hayter.[20] He exhibited at several Paris Salons in 1951, including the Salon d'Hiver, Salon de Mai, and Salon des Jeunes Peintres.[21] He visited contemporary art galleries and museums, including the

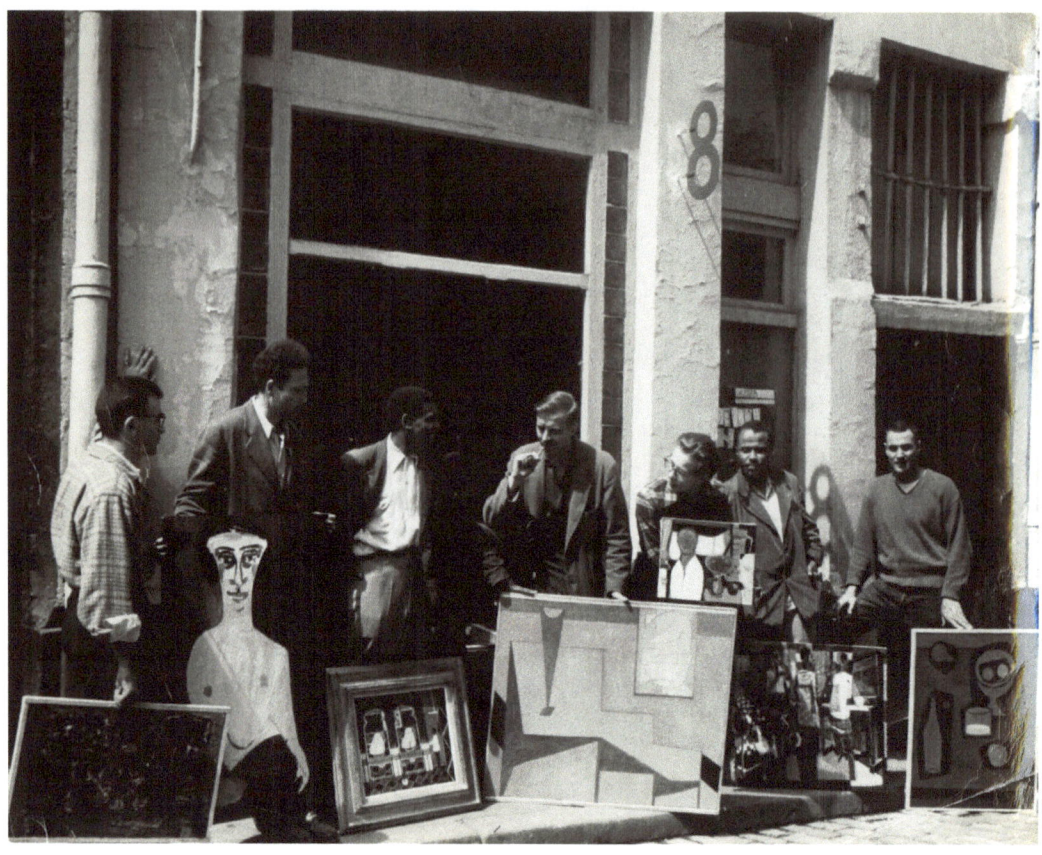

Fig. 4, Paul F. Keene, Jr. at Galerie Huit, Paris, 1950, Photograph. Courtesy of the Keene family.

Louvre, continuing his early interest in Renaissance and Old Master painters.[22] He also spent many hours at the Musée de l'Homme studying African sculpture.[23] Finally, he visited the studios of successful artists such as Pablo Picasso and Fernand Léger, taking advantage of the opportunity to learn from contemporary European Modernists.[24]

The post-war period was an interesting and exciting time to be in Paris. After the end of World War II, many young Americans took the opportunity to travel and study abroad, thanks to the support received from the G.I. Bill. At the same time, many European artists who had fled to the U.S. during the war returned to their homelands, making it easier for their American colleagues to make social connections abroad. Keene later noted that after World War II, things were "heating up" artistically in Paris as well as in New York City.[25] Post-war Paris was also a hotbed for American jazz music, bringing African American musicians to perform in jazz clubs, particularly on the Left Bank around Saint-Germain-des-Prés, with

concerts by legendary performers such as Dizzie Gillespie, Sidney Bechet and Miles Davis.[26]

Keene commented that many African Americans, including himself, went to Paris to "experience freedom," because they felt that there was less racial oppression in France.[27] Legendary Harlem-born author James Baldwin, who travelled to Paris in 1948, eloquently stated that

> African-Americans discover in Paris the terms by which they can define themselves. It's the freedom to work beyond the assumptions of what we can and can't do as African-Americans. It's a different rhythm and pace. We can imagine ourselves in new ways in that space.[28]

In an essay entitled "The Negro in Paris," published in 1950, Baldwin noted that were about 500 African Americans living in Paris at the time, most studying on the G.I. Bill.[29] Art historian Catherine Bernard has argued that African American artists were attracted to France's "mythical status as a country of open-mindedness, hospitality and tolerance," citing a statement made by Lois Mailou Jones, who visited from 1937 to 1938: "France gave me my first feeling of absolute freedom."[30] Many African American artists were inspired by the overseas success of Henry Ossawa Tanner, and travelled to Paris in the hope of escaping the racial oppression prevalent in the U.S.[31]

The exhibition, *Paul Keene: Post-War Explorations in Painting*, features several artworks from Keene's Paris period. These paintings are somber in tone, but with a faceted jewel-like quality and intensity that marked Keene's artistic expression at that time. The influence of Cubism is apparent in paintings such as *Soisy-sous-Montmorency* and *Pietà, Soisy*, both dating to 1951 [cats. 6, 1]. The former is a landscape rendering of the small town in which Keene and his wife lived during their second year in France, located about seven miles north of Paris.[32] The latter painting reflects Keene's ongoing interest in depicting Christian religious imagery, particularly in relation to African American experience. He acknowledged the historically important role of religion in the black community, and thus he would often depict the religious figures in his paintings as African American men and women.[33] Other artworks painted in Paris, like *Mother and Son* (1951) and *Symphony in Blue* (1951) [cats. 2, 3], highlight Keene's continued interest in American Social Realism and in representing African American subjects.

These and other works painted in Paris display a cool palette, with a predominance of blues and grays, and with an expressive use of dark lines. It is tempting to compare Keene's paintings of musicians with Picasso's paintings of street performers from his blue period (1901-1904): in both, figures are rendered with angular features and blue tones suggestive of melancholy and despair. It is more fruitful, I would argue, to compare Keene's artworks of the late 1940s and early 1950s with those of his African American colleagues, such as Charles Alston's *Blues Singer* (c. 1953); Charles Pridgen's *The Blues* (1951); and Elizabeth Catlett's *Blues* (1947), which uses expressive lines and blue colors to emphasize visual connections with blues music. Absorbing the lessons of Social Realism, these and other artists sought to portray African American musicians in engaging and expressive ways to appeal to popular audiences. With *Symphony in Blue*, Keene elongates the bodies of the musicians, particularly the faces and hands, for expressive purposes, using dark outlines to exaggerate figural forms.

While in Paris, Keene began to experiment more with manipulating both color and form for expressive and abstract purposes, directly absorbing the lessons of Cubism and European Modernism. Several paintings in the exhibition, such as *Untitled Abstract* and *Abstract*, both dating to 1951 [cats. 4, 5], highlight Keene's continued interest in abstraction during this time—an interest that would accelerate in the mid-1950s and continue to play an important role in his artistic development.

After studying in Paris for two years, Keene returned briefly to Philadelphia. Then from 1952 to 1954, with support from a John Hay Whitney Foundation Opportunity Fellowship, he lived and worked in Port-au-Prince, Haiti, with his wife and infant son. Initially he had wanted to go to Nigeria, but because of the political turmoil in that country he was unable to get a visa.[34] His alternative choice was to study in Haiti where, he believed, "the African traditions were whole—they hadn't been altered, and the music and all was the same as in Nigeria."[35] Also, he "knew people who knew people in Haiti," through his social connections and family friends, so there would be a support network there for him and his family.[36] Furthermore, he had viewed a recent exhibition of Haitian art, and he was aware that the Haitian Renaissance was in full swing.[37] With his Whitney Fellowship, Keene proposed to study the African roots of Haitian culture, including Voodoo music and dance, and to translate his research into painting.[38] The John Hay Whitney Foundation's Opportunity Fellowships provided minority candidates, like Keene, with the chance to gain professional advancement through travel and study overseas.[39]

During his time in Port-au-Prince, Keene became involved with the Centre d'Art, teaching classes in drawing and in artistic materials to Haitian artists and maintaining a studio space.[40] The Center d'Art was founded by Dewitt Peters, an American conscientious objector during World War II who had gone to Haiti in 1943 to teach English as Alternate Service.[41] Keene later recalled that "We were very fortunate in being with Dewitt and under his wing that we could move on both ends of society.... from the elite to the peasant ith no sweat whatsoever."[42] With Keene's high level of education and fluency in the French language, he and his family were quickly accepted by the Haitian elite, within what was then a very strict class system.[43] During his time at the Centre d'Art, Keene was fortunate to have the opportunity to mingle with artists of different backgrounds, and while

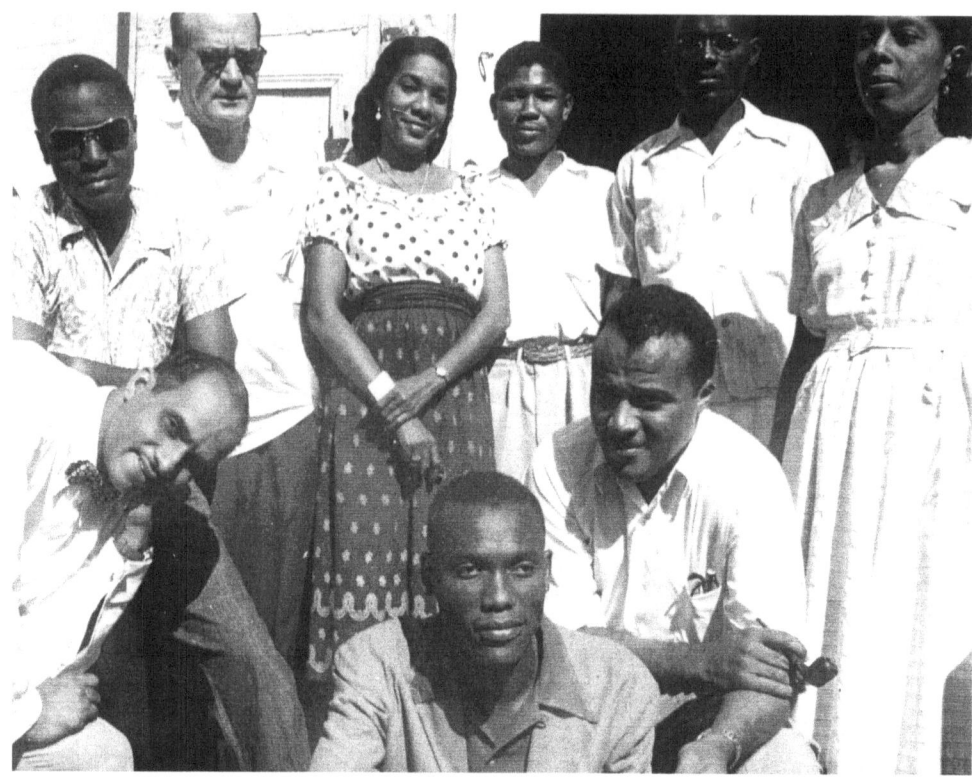

Fig. 5, Paul F. Keene, Jr. at the Centre d'Art, Port-au-Prince, Haiti, 1953, Photograph. Courtesy of the Keene family.

he worked as a painting instructor, he was able to play a role in the Haitian Renaissance through his training and encouragement of local artists.

Keene's experiences in Haiti prompted a major shift in his work, in his use of brighter colors, and also in his interest in Haitian subjects, including scenes from everyday life as well as Voodoo religion. Keene acknowledged the tremendous impact of Haiti on his painting, particularly in his use of intense colors. He later stated, "Everything there was very vibrant and beautiful—the yellows, blues, purples, reds—the light especially was magnificent. I started experimenting with colors...."[44] Thus, paintings such as *Untitled (Abstract)*, completed in Haiti in 1952, present a striking departure from earlier works produced in Paris, such as *Soisy-sous-Montmorency* [cats. 7, 6]. In *Untitled (Abstract)*, sunlit Haitian houses are rendered as solid megalithic constructions rather than as fractured intersecting walls. Here, Keene appears to have abandoned the lessons of Cubism in favor of a more symbolic synthesis of color and form.

Keene developed a close friendship with Haitian artist Antonio Joseph, who had joined the Centre d'Art in

1944.[45] Keene's works were featured in a two-person exhibition with Joseph, which took place at the Centre d'Art in March and April of 1953.[46] Keene exhibited 19 artworks, several of which had recently been purchased by the American collector Joseph H. Hirshhorn. The list of his works on display included scenes of street vendors and chicken sellers, two on the theme of Carnival, and several related to Haitian Voodoo which conveyed spiritual as well as Trinitarian themes, including *Les Trois Tambours, Trois Airs d'Haiti, Trois Guédés*.[47] The cover of the program featured a drawing related to one of Keene's paintings, *Voodoo Priest* (c. 1953) [fig. 6, cat. 12].

While in Haiti, Keene continued to participate in exhibitions in the U.S., shipping paintings to his parents' home in North Philadelphia.[48] Early in 1953, he exhibited at the annual exhibition of the Pennsylvania Academy of the Fine Arts with a painting entitled *Haitian Chicken Vendor* (now *Chicken Woman*), which was later donated to the museum's collection [cat. 8].[49] Around the same time, he was invited to display several works at the Pyramid Club's annual exhibition, for which he received the prestigious 1953 Guest Artist Award. His painting of *Tambourine Girl*, which was in the vein of his earlier

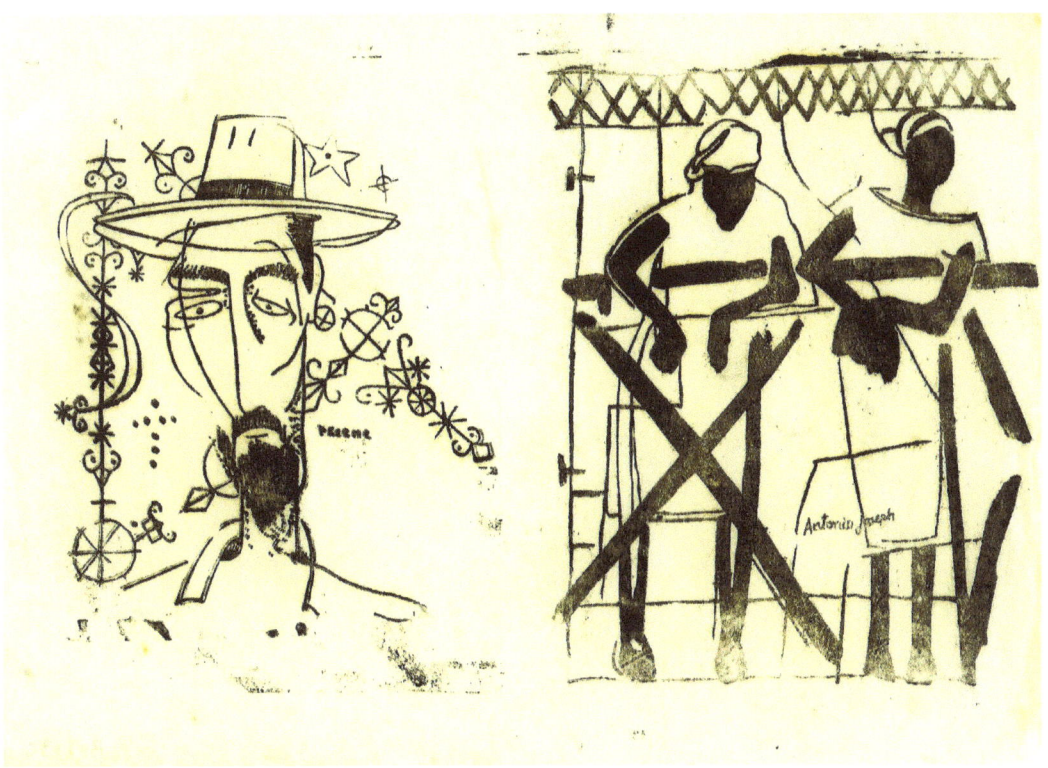

Fig. 6, Cover of Exhibition Program by Paul F. Keene, Jr. (left) and Antonio Joseph (right), Centre d'Art, Port-au-Prince, Haiti, 1953, Relief print on pellum, 6 ¾ x 9 ½ in. Courtesy of the Keene Family and Dolan/Maxwell. Artwork © 2017 Estate of Paul F. Keene, Jr. and Antonio Joseph.

representations of Philadelphia street musicians, was reproduced in the Pyramid Club's exhibition program.[50] Art historian David Brigham has noted the close connections between the Pennsylvania Academy of the Fine Arts and the Pyramid Club during this time period, in their combined efforts to support talented Philadelphia artists.[51]

While some of Keene's artworks from his Haitian period depict local market scenes and everyday life [cats. 8, 9, 10, 14; fig. 7], others such as *Drummer* (1952), *Voodoo Priest* (c. 1953), and *Haitian Voodoo Spirits* (1953) directly evoke Haitian religious subjects, including Voodoo designs and symbols [cats. 11, 12, 23]. Various scholars have noted how Haitian Voodoo, or Vodun, permeates many aspects of Haitian life.[52] As the first independent black republic in the New World, Haiti was established in 1804 in Western Hispaniola following a successful slave revolt. During the 18th century, the ruling class had imported slaves from Central Africa, particularly Congo and Angola, and also from West Africa, from Dahomey, Yoruba, and Igbo, and also Bamana and Mande peoples. Thus, in Haiti, there evolved two main branches of

Vodun: a Kongo/Angola line called Petro-Lemba and a Dahomey/Yoruba line called Rada.[53]

Voodoo was closely intertwined with Catholicism in Haiti, as in other African diasporas, representing a merging of cultural forms from Africa and the New World. Robert Farris Thompson, a noted scholar of African and Afro-Atlantic art, has argued that "vodun is Africa *reblended*."[54] He wrote,

> Everywhere in vodun art one universe abuts another—the gathering of chromolithographs of the saints upon the altar walls; the standing of embottled souls upon the altar dais; the flash of the flags and sword pirouetting around the peristyle; the coming of the deities, responding to this brilliance, through the pillar at the center of the dancing court. Luminous force is caused to extend from the bottom of this pillar in radially disposed, blazing, chalk white blazons of the goddesses and gods. These signs, vèvè, are then erased by the dancing feet of devotees, circling around the pillar, even as, in spirit-possession,

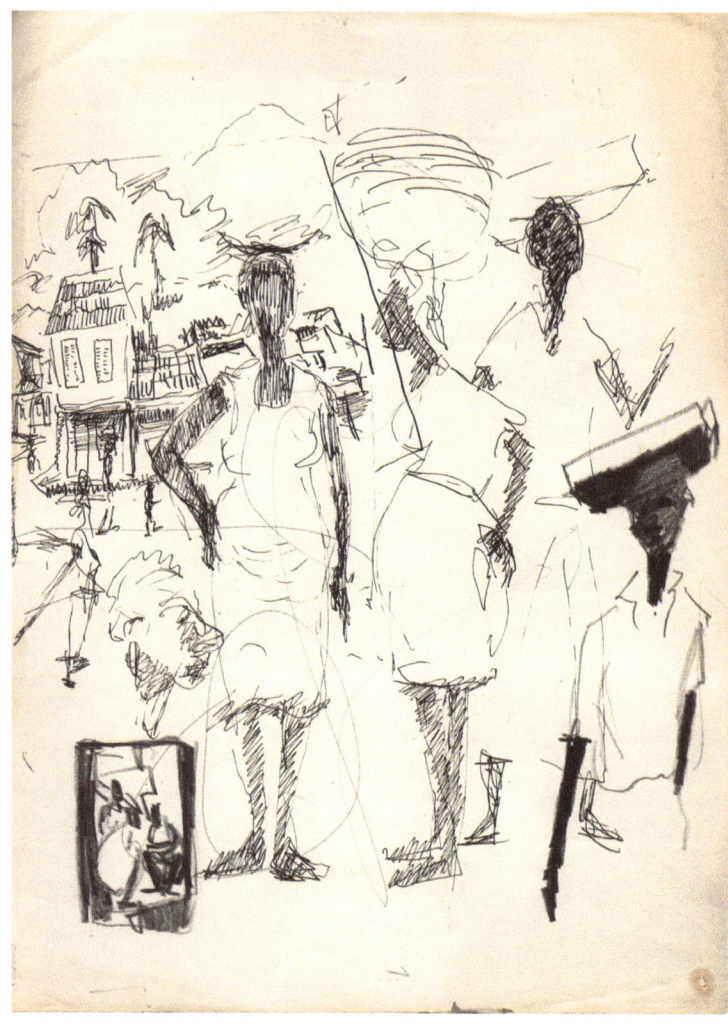

Fig. 7, Paul F. Keene, Jr. (1920-2009), *Haitian Studies*, Ink on Paper, 8 ¾ x 11 ⅞ in., c. 1952. Verso: *Houses at Port-au-Prince*. Courtesy of the Keene Family and Dolan/Maxwell. Artwork © 2017 Estate of Paul F. Keene, Jr.

the figures of these deities are redrawn within their flesh. And then the goddesses and gods themselves revolve around this tree....[55]

Keene's desire to learn about Voodoo rituals stemmed from his long-time interest in religion and also from his ongoing fascination with music, particularly percussion. He later recounted that he would visit Voodoo temples in Haiti and make sketches based on the vèvè patterns on the walls.[56] He also became interested in the links between Voodoo spirituality and other forms of cultural expression which originated in Africa. He was attracted to the element of mystery in Haitian art, what Haitian artists referred to as "Le Mystère," and to the idea of merging history with mysticism, symbolism and myth.[57]

A major masterpiece from Keene's Haitian period is *Haitian Voodoo Spirits* (1953) [cat. 23]. Here he portrayed Voodoo subject matter in a triptych format, like the kind often used for Christian religious paintings. He also represented several sets of threes in the painting, evoking Trinitarian themes, and he incorporated vèvè patterns in all of the panels. The left panel depicts three drummers, presided over by a vèvè symbol which represents a Voodoo *houngan*.[58] The central panel presents three glowing heads in the lower half of the composition, and above this is a vèvè drawing of two snakes connected on a base, representing Damballah and Aida Wédo, the male and female primary gods of the vodun pantheon, facing in towards an almond- or egg-shaped design [fig. 8].[59] The right panel presents three drummers, with their heads at descending heights, seated above a large decorated vessel.

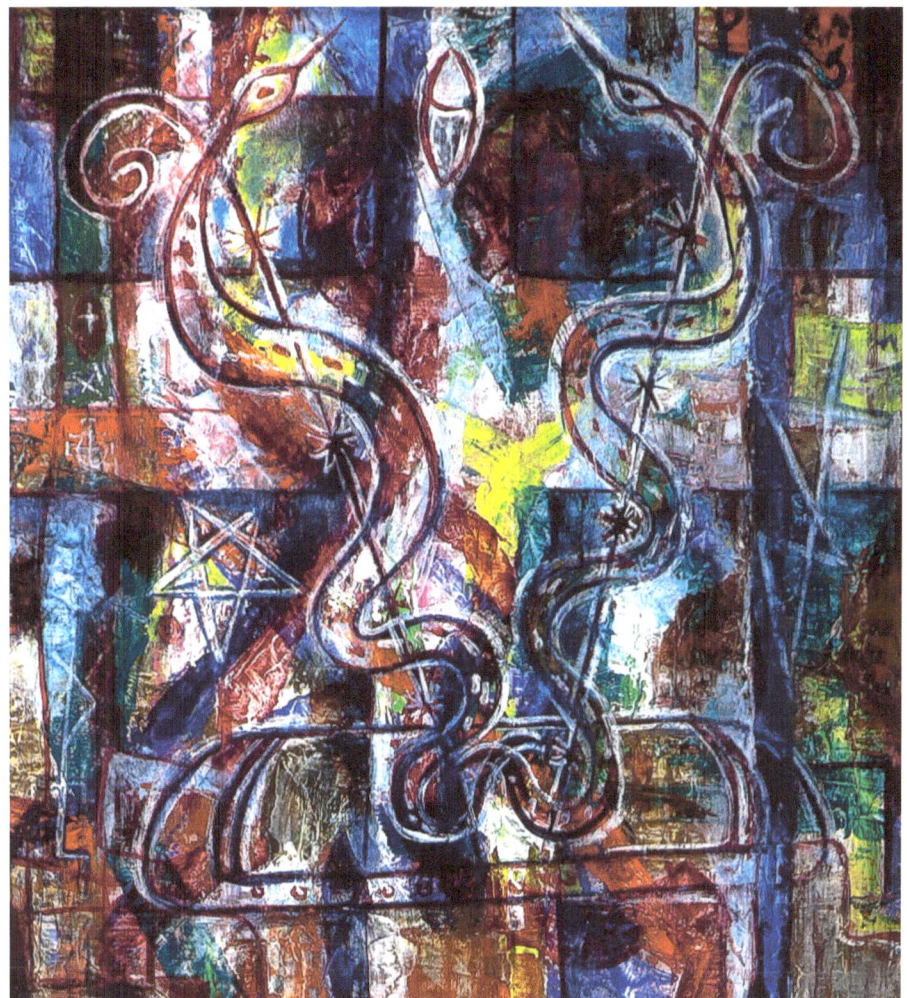

Fig. 8, Paul F. Keene, Jr. (1920-2009), *Haitian Voodoo Spirits* (Detail of Central Panel), 1953, Oil on Wood Panels, 69 ¼ x 80 in. (total), Collection of La Salle University Art Museum, Gift of Benjamin D. Bernstein, 01-P-474(1-3). Artwork © 2017 Estate of Paul F. Keene, Jr. and La Salle University Art Museum.

On the far right side of the panel is a vertical vèvè pattern of three circular cruciform designs, with the middle circle intersecting with the drummer's halo. The particular vèvè pattern signifies drums and an ogan (a kind of iron cymbal), and may suggest the sequence of drum beats in a prominent Voodoo ritual.[60] In his triptych, Keene represents Haitian musicians engaged in a Voodoo ritual, overlaid with actual vèvè designs scratched into the surface of the painting, combined with Christian symbols of the Trinity and the Crucifixion.

The central panel, with its presentation of the symbols of the two primary Voodoo gods, is suggestive of the experience and focus of important Haitian Voodoo rituals. In her ethnographic book, *Divine Horsemen: The Living Gods of Haiti* (published in 1953, the same year that the painting was created), Maya Deren described the god Damballah as an ancient, venerable and wise father. "He is shown as a snake, arched in the path that the sun travels across the sky; sometime half the arch is composed of his female counterpart, Ayida, the rainbow."[61] She noted that "Damballah and Ayida, who together represent the sexual totality, encompass the cosmos as a serpent coiled around the world. The egg, the world egg, is the special symbol for them; and an egg is the particular offering to Damballah."[62] She also explained that during Voodoo ceremonies invoking the god Damballah, "the drums and the chorus surge forward with such solid sound, such deep fullness, as rarely marks the invocation to any other deity."[63]

In this painting, Keene includes patterns which originate from the elaborate vèvè designs in Haitian Voodoo temples. As Thompson explained, "The celebrated blazons, vèvè, are traced in powdered substances (usually corn meal) upon the earth about the central column of the vodun dancing-court, the *poteau-mitan*. Symmetrically disposed and fashioned, vèvè praise, summon, and incarnate, all at once, the deities of the vodun pantheon."[64] These vèvè patterns ultimately derive from Fon and Kongo traditions of sacred ground painting in Africa. They often have a cruciform structure, with a central axis and four radiating arms, which, as Thompson noted, "seem linked to the rhetorical impetus of the Kongo cosmogram, drawn, like vèvè, on the earth to indicate, in serious settings (oath-taking, spirit-possession, initiation, and so forth), the boundary between the two worlds and the moral watchfulness of God and the dead."[65] Keene's incorporation of vèvè patterns in his paintings not only references Haitian Voodoo symbolism and its African origins, but also functions as a way of highlighting the surface of the painting, the boundary between his painted visions and their reception by his viewers.

Keene's experiences abroad, in Paris and particularly in Haiti, contributed to his professional success when he returned to the U.S. In 1954 he had a one-person show at the Dubin Gallery in Philadelphia and sold all 33 paintings on display.[66] He also exhibited work in a group show of Whitney Fellowship recipients, from which John Hay Whitney bought two of his paintings.[67] In December 1954, he was the subject of a *Philadelphia Tribune* newspaper article, which hailed him as an outstanding new talent and noted his inclusion in an *Art in America* feature on "Artists with a Future."[68] He taught at the Philadelphia College of Art from 1954 to 1968, achieving the rank of associate professor; then he taught at Bucks County Community College in Newtown, PA, where he helped to establish the art department.[69]

During the mid-1950s, Keene continued to exhibit paintings that featured Philadelphia street scenes; but he also exhibited paintings representing Haitian subject matter, some created in Haiti, along with new works which drew upon his memories of the island nation and its people. His paintings from this period also demonstrate his continued oscillation between figuration and abstraction. This is illustrated by contrasting works such as *Clarinet Player* (1955), in which Keene rendered a clearly-defined figure of a black musician in an urban setting; and *The Sorceress* (1956), in which he used predominantly bright red colors and abstract markings to portray a Haitian Voodoo priestess [cats. 17, 16].

While Keene continued to evoke Haitian themes in his work, he appeared to become increasingly interested in the layering and distillation of colors. In paintings such as *The Altered Ego* (c. 1955) and *Baroque Warriors* (1957), Keene filled the canvases with abstract figural forms, with elongated necks and haloed heads, suggestive of human beings, or perhaps their spiritual counterparts [cats. 21, 22]. The figures seem to emerge from or dissolve in thick dabs of paint, creating the abstract symphonies of color and form.

Keene also painted overtly religious images such as *Horseman of the Apocalypse* (1956), a subject resonant with both Christian symbolism and Haitian mythology [cat. 18]. By giving the painting this title, Keene encouraged viewers to interpret the image in relation to the New Testament Book of Revelations (6:1-8), an apocalyptic text describing the breaking of seven symbolic seals heralding the Second Coming of Christ. The opening of the first four seals would release four fearsome horses with riders, the first a white horse bent on conquest, followed by red and black horses bringing war and famine. Keene's painting appears to depict the fourth horseman, a pale horse ridden by the figure of Death. Interestingly, this dynamic image of a horse and its bareback rider viewed from the rear, twisting and turning, has its roots in a preliminary sketch dating to 1950 [fig. 9]. Keene's exploration of this theme may also allude to the popular Voodoo idea of the possessed individuals as divine horsemen—an idea explored by Deren in her book, *Divine Horsemen*, cited above.

As Keene's career progressed, he continued to explore his interest in spirituality and in religious parables, legends, and myths. His paintings from his Paris and Haiti years paved the way for his later portrayals of myths and legends of the black community, as in his Root Man series of the 1960s, and his Myths and Legends series of the 1980s.[70] Keene also continued to explore his longstanding fascination with the theme of death, and the mysticism associated with death—later noting that the theme ran through all of his work, possibly due to his childhood experiences growing up in a funeral home.[71] While Keene's interest in universal and mythic elements, and in mysticism, connects his work with post-war international Modernist currents, his paintings from the late 1940s

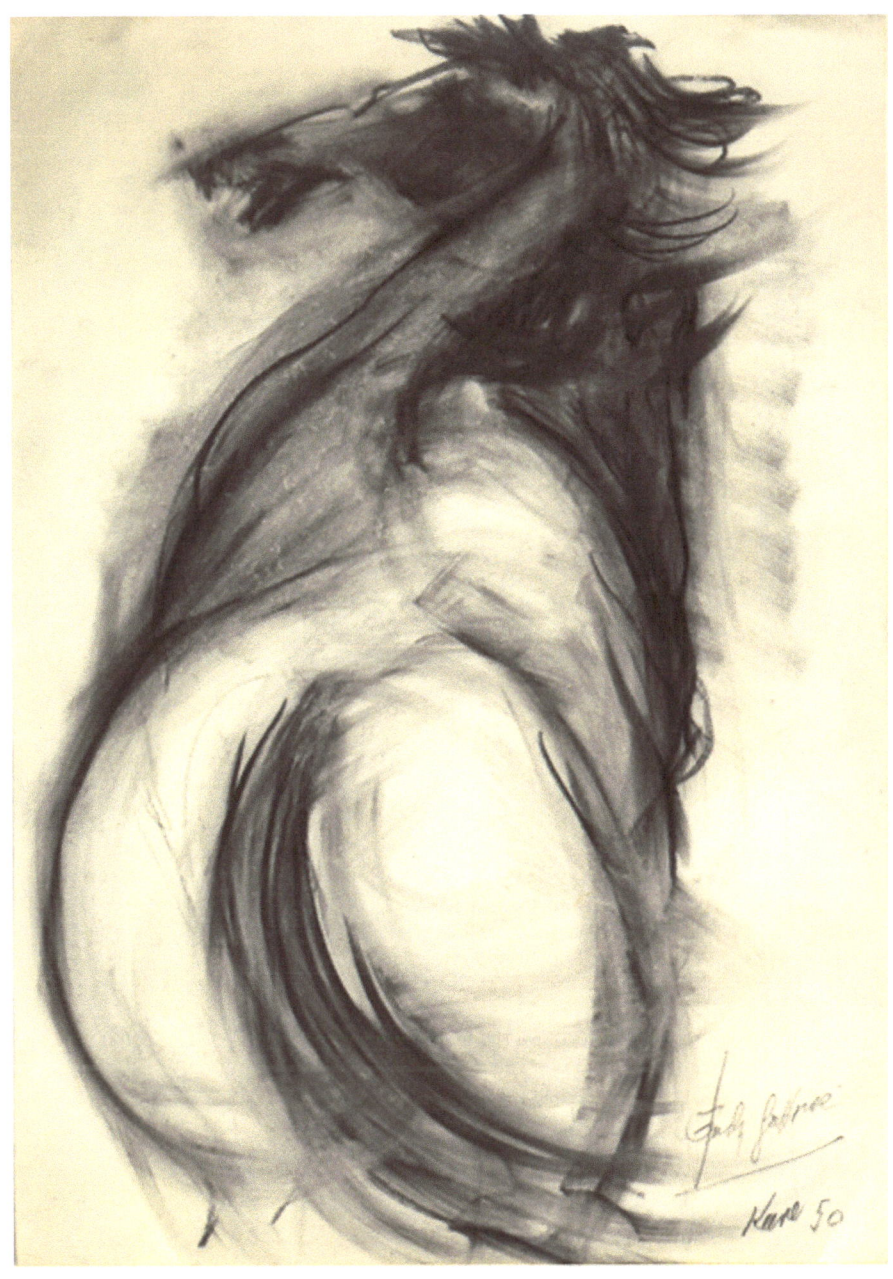

Fig. 9, Paul F. Keene, Jr. (1920-2009), Preliminary Sketch for *Horseman of the Apocalypse*, 1950, 10¾ x 12¾ in., Courtesy of the Keene Family and Dolan/Maxwell. Artwork © 2017 Estate of Paul F. Keene, Jr.

through the late 1950s also demonstrate his continued interest of figuration, and in what he called "figurative abstractions," particularly with regard to representing African American subjects. As he oscillated between figuration and abstraction, and strived to combine both forms of artistic expression, he expressed a life-long commitment to celebrating the both social and spiritual aspects of black cultural life.[72]

Klare Scarborough, Ph.D.
Director and Chief Curator,
La Salle University Art Museum

1   Curlee Raven Holton, "Paul Keene: A Life as an Artist," in *Paul Keene: His Art and His Legacy*, ed. Curlee Raven Holton (Doylestown: James A. Michener Art Museum, 2005), 21-73.

2   Bonnie L. Cook, "Paul Farwell Keene Jr., 1920- 2009, Acclaimed Artist's Works Raised Racial Awareness," *The Philadelphia Inquirer*, December 13, 2009.

3   Marina Pacini, *Oral History Interview with Paul Keene*, 1990 Apr. 23, Selected Interview Transcripts from the Oral History Collection of the Archives of American Art (No. 17), Smithsonian Institution, 1-152, esp. 6-9.

4   Pacini, *Oral History Interview*, 18-22. See also Cook, "Paul Farwell Keene Jr."

5   Keene's diplomas are included in the *Paul F. Keene Papers*, [ca. 1940]-1987, Archives of American Art, Smithsonian Institution.

6   Ibid., 37-39. For more on the Pyramid Club, see David R. Brigham, "Dox Thrash and the Pyramid Club," in *Dox Thrash: An African American Master Printmaker Rediscovered*, ed. John Ittman (Philadelphia: Philadelphia Museum of Art, and Seattle: University of Washington Press, 2001), pp. 53-63, 159-161; Woodmere Art Museum, *We Speak: Black Artists in Philadelphia, 1920s-1970s* (Philadelphia: Woodmere Art Museum, 2016), esp. 16-17, 158-165, 166-173; and Kia Gregory, "Legacy of a Clubhouse; Philly's Pyramid Club, a beloved, revered hangout for black professionals," *The Philadelphia Inquirer* (February 11, 2010).

7   Holton, "Paul Keene," 21-25. See also Lewis Tanner Moore, "Paul Keene and the Philadelphia Tradition: Reflections by Lewis Tanner Moore," in *Paul Keene: His Art and His Legacy*, ed. Curlee Raven Holton (Doylestown: James A. Michener Art Museum, 2005), 16-18; and David R. Brigham, "The Pyramid Club and the Pennsylvania Academy of Fine Arts," *Antiques and Fine Art Magazine*, 2008, http://www.antiquesandfineart.com/articles/article.cfm?request=912. See also Alain Locke, *Negro Art: Past and Present* (Washington: Associates in Negro Folk Education, 1936); and Alain Locke, ed., *The Negro in Art: A Pictorial Record of the Negro Artist and of the Negro Theme in Art* (Washington: Associates in Negro Folk Education, 1940). For Allan Freelon's views, see Allan Freelon, "Modern Negro Art, *Journal of Negro Education* 13, no. 2 (April 1944): 203, a book review of James A. Porter, *Modern Negro Art* (New York: Dryden Press, 1943); Woodmere Art Museum, *We Speak: Black Artists in Philadelphia, 1920s-1970s*, esp. 126-145; Kenneth G. Rodgers, *Allan Freelon: Pioneer African American Impressionist* (Durham, NC: North Carolina Central University Art Museum, 2004); and Jim Weaver, "Allan Freelon: Pioneer African-American Impressionist: September 19 - November 28, 2004," Woodmere Art Museum, Traditional Fine Arts Organization, http://www.tfaoi.com/aa/4aa/4aa566.htm.

8   Keene's association with American Scene painting was noted by contemporary reviewers as well as later historians. See Walter E. Baum, "Closeups on Art: American Scene is Pictured in Show at Alliance," *The Sunday Bulletin*, Philadelphia, November 28, 1948 [included in the Paul F. Keene Papers]. See also Holton, "Paul Keene," 24.

9   Pacini, *Oral History Interview*, 40.

10 Pacini, *Oral History Interview*, 78-80.

11 Ibid., 40-42.

12 Ibid., 85, 87.

13 C.H. Bonte, "Famous Artists Exhibiting in Pyramid Club's Annual," *The Philadelphia Inquirer*, Sunday, February 22, 1948 [included in the *Paul F. Keene Papers*].

14 Pacini, *Oral History Interview*, 87-88.

15 Serge Guilbaut, ed., *Reconstructing Modernism: Art in New York, Paris, and Montreal, 1945-1964* (Cambridge: MIT Press, c. 1990). See also Serge Guilbaut, *How New York Stole the Idea of Modern Art: Abstract Expressionism, Freedom, and the Cold War*, trans. Arthur Goldhammer (Chicago: University of Chicago Press, 1983); and Jed Perl, ed., *Art in America 1945-1970: Writings from the Age of Abstract Expressionism, Pop Art, and Minimalism* (New York: Library of America, 2014).

16 Pacini, *Oral History Interview*, 28-30, 76.

17 Ibid., 30-33. See also Holton, "Paul Keene," 30.

18 Pacini, *Oral History Interview*, 43-44.

19 Ibid., 51-53. For information about Galerie Huit and the post-war art scene in Paris, see Audreen Buffalo, ed., *Explorations in the City of Light : African-American Artists in Paris, 1945-1965* (New York: Studio Museum in Harlem, 1996); and exhibition review by Michael Kimmelman, "Art View: Black Artists at Home in Postwar Paris," *The New York Times* (February 8, 1996). See also the exhibition catalogue, *Galerie Huit: American Artists in Paris 1950-52* (New York: Studio 18 Gallery, 2002); and the exhibition review by Lewis Tanner Moore, "Revisiting Post-War Paris," *International Review of African American Art* 18, no. 4 (2002): 61-62. Finally, see Michael David Plante, *The "Second Occupation": American Expatriate Painters and the Reception of American Art in Paris, 1946-58*, Ph.D. Dissertation, History of Art, Brown University, 1992.

20 Pacini, *Oral History Interview*, 56, 60-61.

21 Ibid, 49.

22 Ibid., 8, 76.

23 Ibid., 77-78. Prior to his time in Paris, Keene also studied African art first-hand at the University of Pennsylvania Museum of Archaeology and Anthropology and at the Philadelphia Commercial Museum.

24 Ibid., 58-59, 63.

25 Ibid., 62.

26 Tyler Stovall, "African American Artists Return to Paris" and "Jazz in Saint-Germain-des-Prés," in *Be-Bomb: the Transatlantic War of Images and All That Jazz, 1946-1956*, eds. Serge Guilbaut and Manuel J. Borja-Villel (Barcelona: Museu d'Art Contemporani de Barcelona; Madrid: Museo Nacional Centro de Arte Reina Sofía, 2007), 105-121; 122-137. For more on jazz in post-war Paris, see Rashida K. Braggs, *Jazz Diasporas: Race, Music and Migration in Post-World War II Paris* (Oakland: University of California Press, 2016).

27 Pacini, *Oral History Interview*, 62.

28 Cited in Maureen Jenkins, "African-Americans in Paris: It's Always Been About Freedom for Us," CNN Travel (Feb 26, 2013), http://www.cnn.com/2013/02/25/travel/paris-african-american-history-tours/.

29 James Baldwin, "The Negro in Paris," *The Reporter* (June 6, 1950), 34-36, esp. 34.

30 Catherine Bernard, "Confluence: Harlem Renaissance, Modernism and Negritude. Paris in the 1920s-1930s," in *Explorations in the City of Light: African-American Artists in Paris, 1945-1965*, ed. Audreen Buffalo (New York: Studio Museum in Harlem, 1996), 21-27, esp. 21; 27, n. 6. She cites her interview with Lois Mailou Jones on June 4, 1994.

31 Ibid., 21-22.

32 Pacini, *Oral History Interview*, 46-48; Holton, "Paul Keene," 31.

33 Pacini, *Oral History Interview*, 84-85.

34 Ibid., 92-95.

35 Ibid., 96.

36 Ibid.

37 Ibid., 97-98.

38 Ibid., 98.

39 Esther Raushenbush, *John Hay Whitney Foundation: A Report of the First Twenty-Five Years*, Vol. 1 (New York: John Hay Whitney Foundation, 1972).

40 Pacini, *Oral History Interview*, 99-102.

41 Pierre Monosiet, "A Chronology of Haitian Art," in *Haitian Art*, ed. Ute Stebich (New York: The Brooklyn Museum and Henry N. Abrams, Inc., 1978), 12-17, esp. 14.

42 Pacini, *Oral History Interview*, 105.

43 Ibid.

44 Paul Keene, Interview with Lewis Tanner Moore, 2007. Cited in the Press Release for the Noyes Museum of Art exhibition of *Paul Keene: Impressions of the Shore*, August 27, 2007.

45 Joseph later became the first Haitian artist to receive a prestigious Guggenheim Fellowship. Pacini, *Oral History Interview*, 102; Monosiet, "A Chronology of Haitian Art," 12-13.

46 *Le Centre d'Art 100th Exhibition: Paul Keene, Antonio Joseph* (March 19 - April 5, 1953), Exhibition Program [included in the *Paul F. Keene Papers*].

47 Ibid.

48 Invoice of Merchandise dated January 8, 1953, included in the *Paul F. Keene Papers*.

49 *Catalogue of the One Hundred and Forty-Eighth Annual Exhibition of Painting and Sculpture*, The Pennsylvania Academy of the Fine Arts (January 25-March 1, 1953) [included in the *Paul Keene F. Papers*].

50 Letter from Humbert Howard to Paul Keene dated February 11, 1953; and *Catalogue of the Thirteenth Annual Exhibition of The Pyramid Club* [both included in the *Paul F. Keene Papers*]. See also Gertrude Benson, "Pyramid Club Gives Annual Art Show," *The Philadelphia Inquirer*, Sunday, March 1, 1953.

51 Brigham, "The Pyramid Club and the Pennsylvania Academy of the Fine Arts."

52 See Sheldon Williams, *Voodoo and the Art of Haiti* (Nottingham: Morland Lee Ltd., 1969); Michel S. Laguerre, *Voodoo Heritage* (Beverly Hills and London: Sage Publications, 1980); and Michel S. Laguerre, *Voodoo and Politics in Haiti* (New York: St. Martin's Press, 1989).

53 Robert Farris Thompson, "The Flash of the Spirit: Haiti's Africanizing Vodun Art," in *Haitian Art*, ed. Ute Stebich (New York: The Brooklyn Museum and Henry N. Abrams, Inc., 1978), 26-37, esp. 26.

54 Thompson, "The Flash of the Spirit," 26.

55 Ibid., 34-35.

56 Pacini, *Oral History Interview*, 111.

57 Paul Keene, "Haitian Painters," *Artists Equity Association Newsletter, Philadelphia Chapter*, Vol. 2, No. 1 (July 1954) [reprinted later in this book]. See also Pacini, *Oral History Interview*, 103-104.

58 For an illustration and analysis of this vèvè symbol, see *Milo Rigaud, La Tradition Voodoo et le Voodoo Haitien (Son Temple, Ses Mystères, Sa Magie)* (Paris: Editions Niclaus, 1953), 363.

59 Ibid., 316-322.

60 Maya Deren, *Divine Horsemen: The Living Gods of Haiti* (London and New York: Thames and Hudson, 1953), 234-235. Deren also filmed voodoo rituals in Haiti, starting in 1947 and continuing through 1954, the footage of which was later edited and produced as a posthumous documentary film, *Divine Horsemen: The Living Gods of Haiti*, in 1977. For more about Deren's work, see Bill Nichols, ed., *Maya Deren and the American Avant-Garde* (Berkeley, Los Angeles and London: University of California Press, 2001).

61 Deren, *Divine Horsemen*, 115.

62 Ibid., 116.

63 Ibid.

64 Thompson, "The Flash of the Spirit," 33.

65 Ibid., 29.

66 Pacini, *Oral History Interview*, 112. Many of Keene's paintings were purchased by Philadelphia collector Benjamin D. Bernstein, who later donated works to local educational institutions such as La Salle University Art Museum, Villanova University, Woodmere Art Museum, and the Pennsylvania Academy of the Fine Arts. Ibid., 151.

67 Ibid., 109-110.

68 "Museum School of Art Instructor Exhibited Both in U.S., Europe," *The Philadelphia Tribune*, December 14, 1954. For Keene's inclusion in "Artists with a Future," see Adelyn D. Breeskin, "Middle Atlantic States," *Art in America* 43 (Feb. 1955): 32-35, esp. 34.

69 Pacini, *Oral History Interview*, 119. See also Cook, "Paul Farwell Keene Jr."

70 Ibid., 135-136. See also Leslie King-Hammond, *Masters on the Cutting Edge: Icons, Myths, and Legends; Paul F. Keene Jr.* (Philadelphia: African American Museum in Philadelphia; Doylestown: James A. Michener Art Museum, 1991).

71 Pacini, *Oral History Interview*, 125-127.

72 Ibid., 84-86.

Paul Keene and the Haitian Experience

Haitian culture, history and artists alike have influenced Philadelphia-born artist, Paul Farwell Keene Jr., in a plethora of ways. His works of the early 1950s exhibit motifs, styles and themes that are often associated with Haitian art. The themes found in Keene's artworks also serve as a signifier of an Afro-Modernity engaged in the search for a "primitive" Afro-centric expression, and the Caribbean artistic avant-garde style often evinced in Haitian art. Alongside Haitian and American pioneers such as Robert St. Brice, Antonio Joseph, Jason Seley and DeWitt Peters, Keene mentored numerous artists in Haiti while incorporating new techniques and visual allusions to the Haitian experience in his work.

It was in August of 1952 that Paul Keene received a fellowship from the John Hay Whitney Foundation, which allowed him to study and teach in Haiti. He had been to Paris already and was interested in studying Afro-Modernity in Africa. Derailed by travel bureaucracy and logistics, he settled on travel to Haiti upon the advice of friends and colleagues who helped provide contact information. Haiti promised to offer a similar experience as it was often referred to as the "Africa of the Americas." Keene was aware that the Haitian Renaissance was happening but later admitted that he was only vaguely familiar with Haitian art at the time. It was his professional connections, especially his acquaintance with DeWitt Peters, which helped solidify Keene's plans to go to Haiti. He was looking forward to learning new ways to translate dance and music into his paintings.

Prior to Keene's embarkation to Haiti, he had focused on mostly figurative work that dealt with being black and with black culture. He was heavily involved in the jazz scene in Philadelphia, which became a strong presence in his work. Even so, religious and mythological themes become an important part of his work as well, albeit in a subconscious way. As a youth, Keene grew up in a funeral home and embedded himself in the church as an altar boy, but he later severed ties with organized religion. Nonetheless, many artists, critics and viewers have noted religious imagery in his work. Some paintings done by Keene that exhibit religious imagery include *Jacob and the Angel* and *Horseman of the Apocalypse*

[cat. 18]. Keene was also very interested in parables, legends and myths. He found them all to be fascinating. Naturally, the dream-like quality often found in Haitian paintings infused with Voodoo spirituality and imagery also found its way into Keene's work. Haiti was a place where Keene could experience relatively unaltered African traditions—music, drums, carvings and culture. The naïve, so-called primitive style of Haitian art often captured how Haitians portrayed their culture. Their art syncretized Catholicism, freemasonry, and Voodoo, with brilliant colors and local scenes.

In Haiti, Keene taught informal art classes for two years at the Centre d'Art in Port-au-Prince and influenced young native painters who had little or no formal art education and training. Many of these artists resided in the countryside and were found by DeWitt Peters, Jason Seley, Keene and the artists involved in the Centre d'Art in Port-au-Prince. They spent a lot of time in the 1950s and 1960s searching for naturally-gifted Haitian artists in order to give them artistic training and opportunities, and thus provide them with a livelihood. However, the Centre d'Art was more than that—it was a social hub for the arts in Port-au-Prince. Grand exhibitions, shows and theatre groups gathered there frequently, making the Centre d'Art an exciting place. The Haitian Renaissance also led to a constant demand of Haitian art by visitors from all over the world; thus, the Centre d'Art became a place to make international connections. It was through the Centre d'Art that Keene sold many works to collectors like Joseph H. Hirshhorn and John Hay Whitney.

Even though Keene spent two years working with Haitian artists and teaching the technical aspects of painting, he claimed that Haitian artists had a greater impact on his work than he had on theirs. His interactions with Haitian artists like Antonio Joseph, who studied with him, began to influence the content and intensity of his own work. Keene noted that one of the reasons he went to Haiti was because he was "always hung up on that kind of mysticism, the legends and the myths, and where reality stops and other begins and vice versa." He remarked that, stylistically his work did not consciously change. While Haitian art itself had an impact on Keene's work, it was

Fig. 10, George Liautaud (1899-1991), *Cross*, c. 1953, Iron. Collection of Laura Keene. © 2017 Estate of George Liautaud

more so the cultural experience of living in Haiti which was often echoed in his paintings.

Haitian art is noticeably original, vibrant and eye-catching. The paintings and imagery are rich in representations of Haitian culture, and Keene absorbed it all. The use of color fascinated him most and was important to Keene in his work, as he was a self-considered colorist. He had a visceral love of color that he used to illuminate stories and different aspects of black culture. Similarly, the artists in Haiti painted vibrantly colorful works to share their experiences. Haitian artists' expressive representations of their culture and interesting use of color seemed, in part, to emanate from the complex and religious Voodoo traditions on the island. According to Keene, Haitian art was an integration of Haiti's history, myth and religion. In the age of Afro-Modernity, the so-called primitive and naïve style of self-taught Haitian artists reflected not only their pride and idealist views but also unadulterated depictions of what was seen and

what was known. Keene found the work produced by the Haitian artists around him to be interesting, mysterious, and not optically realistic—terms that could also be used to describe his own work around this time.

While Keene was in Haiti he collected and acquired paintings by many Haitian artists that he either worked with or taught at the Centre d'Art. He collected artwork by Antonio Joseph, Philomé Obin, Préfète Duffaut and George Liautaud. In fact, Keene can be credited with discovering George Liautaud and was especially influential in shaping his success. Liautaud's work become internationally collected and known through his connection with the Centre d'Art where he met Keene and other notable artists. Liautaud was an artist who focused solely on metal sculptures, originally iron crosses for graveyards. Seeing Liautaud's iron crosses made Keene think about different possibilities for creating new pieces of art [figs. 10, 11].

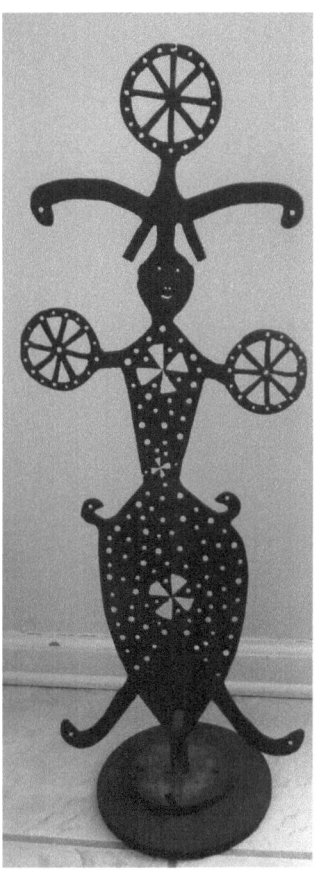

Fig. 11, George Liautaud (1899-1991) and Paul F. Keene, Jr.
(1920-2009), *Haitian Figure*, c. 1953, Iron. Collection of
Laura Keene. Artwork © 2017 Estate of George Liautaud and
Paul F. Keene, Jr.

The Voodoo temples in Haiti were of great interest to Keene, and he would often go there and sketch some of the inspiring imagery that was on the walls. He showed his sketches to Liautaud and asked if he could sculpt the designs using metal. Through the sculpture that Liautaud made for Keene, tourists began to take immediate notice of his iron work and offered to buy the piece before he could even present it to Keene. This sparked a new shift in Liautaud's career as he began churning out sculptures depicting different Voodoo Loas and popular Voodoo spirits.

Préfète Duffaut is another well-known Haitian artist that Keene admired and collected. He joined the Centre d'Art in 1948 and is renowned for the naïve style of his paintings, which often featured hallucinatory landscapes, mysticism, Voodoo subjects, and coastal landscapes of his hometown, Jacmel. Keene collected one of Duffaut's "Villes Imaginaires," which was part of a series of imaginary cities [fig. 12]. In this painting, the vibrant fantastical

landscape is a utopia populated by mountainous terrain, trees, winding roads and city infrastructure. As often noted in Duffaut's work, there is also a coastal element to the painting. The fanciful cityscape imagery, geometric lines and striking colors appealed to Keene during his stay on the island.

Keene's time in Haiti ultimately allowed him to sate his curiosity and explore Haitian religion and everyday life. Voodoo traditions and a celebratory primitivism were the basis from which many Haitian artists drew inspiration. During his two brief years Keene gained a deeper understanding of the urban anxieties as well as the vibrant beauty that characterized Haiti. His work was partly shaped by his experiences in Haiti, which provided the fundamental links that he was seeking to African culture.

Many of Keene's works, especially those painted between 1952 and 1954, such as *Haitian Voodoo Spirits* and

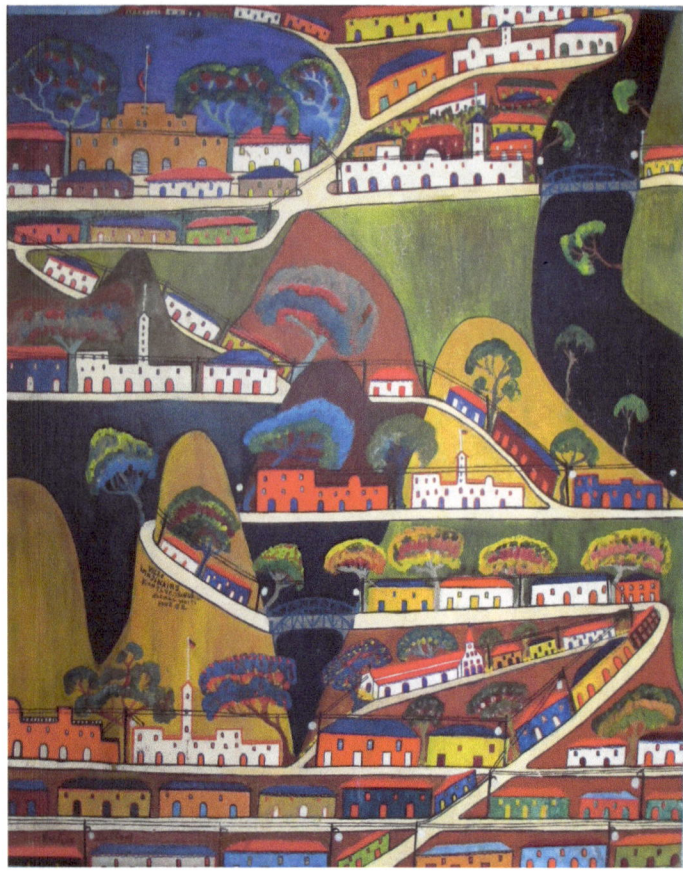

Fig. 12, Préfète Duffaut, Ville Imaginare, 1952, Oil on Board. Collection of Laura Keene. Artwork © 2017 Estate of Préfète Duffaut.

Voodoo Priest, contain references to Haitian art and culture, especially Voodoo spirituality. Even some of his abstract and textured paintings reveal new perspectives and color usage as a direct influence of Haiti. Not only did Keene benefit from his exploration of Haitian culture but he also helped raise the visibility of Haitian art during his time there. Under DeWitt Peters' wing, Keene was able to seamlessly move on both ends of society; and they used their American connections to increase the international awareness of Haitian art.

Bianca Desamour
La Salle University, Class of 2016

Sources

Holton, Curlee Raven, ed. (2005). *Paul Keene: His Art and His Legacy*. Doylestown: James A. Michener Art Museum.

Keene, Laura. (2016), Conversation with the Author.

Pacini, M. (1990). *Oral History Interview with Paul Keene*, 1990 Apr. 23 [Microfilm]. Archives of American Art, Smithsonian Institution, 1-152.

Paul F. Keene Papers, [ca. 1940]-1987 (1988). [Microfilm]. Archives of American Art, Smithsonian Institution.

Twa, L.J. (2014). *Visualizing Haiti in U.S. Culture: 1910-1950*. Farnham: Ashgate.

Stebich, U. (1978). *Haitian Art*. New Orleans Museum of Art, Milwaukee Art Center, and Brooklyn Museum. New York: Brooklyn Museum and H. N. Abrams.

Haitian Painters

In considering the Haitian painter, I concentrate on an important quality that has certainly been noticed by writers, but never fully exploited – the Haitian psychic insight which has for its basis the beauty of his recognition of "Le Mystère" and the dark poetry of his religion expressed in terms of painting. Because of an innate color sense that tends to dominate his paintings, this quality is generally somewhat submerged.

The art of the Haitian evolves in the changing habits of the deities – the spiritual quantity which prompts most artistic expression, regardless of nationality or culture. Art in their case is more than anything else an expression of their belief in native customs and folkways.

Religion and art for the Haitian painter are segments of life never to be considered separately. The vital purpose of artistic expression for him is to represent and mirror with common appeal that unseen world of spirits and to show these spirits in their separate, active characters and identities. The spirits are the controlling factors for the well-being of man in the natural and supernatural worlds. He is at all times in contact with the pantheon of deities which exists in his dual religion. I say "dual" because it involves all the mysteries of Christian and pagan religious fervor.

The Haitian is able to identify and align himself intimately with either the unseen world or the one in which he actively lives. All the painter's responses to life are creative ones; the most trivial experience is of great significance. The discovery of the value of his own ethnic background and its relationship to the society in which he lives has a great effect on the Haitian. It sends him straight through life revealing his world unerringly, without fear and with utmost confidence. Every effort he makes comes from deep within himself and at times his only explanation for that which he has produced is "Le Mystère."

There are instances of paintings being the result of direct commands from some God who ordered the artist to paint specific subjects. And, too, there have been occasions when a God or Saint has aided and guided the hand of the artist in the completion of a major work.

The active presence of supernatural forces and powers is an accepted fundamental and religious concept. It endows all objects, animate or inanimate, and is a life force both potential and actively dynamic. This power serves as a liaison between the supernatural and natural worlds while permeating all thought and matter the artist concerns himself with.

This psychic insight of the Haitian is revealed with dynamic clarity in the works of men like Joseph Bigaud, Benoit, Bazile and Gorgue. No instance of their art can be confused with that of Europe, America, Asia, or—oddly enough—Africa. The popular art movement in Haiti is relatively a pure one, born free of schools and existing painting traditions.

Paul F. Keene, Jr.

Reprinted from the *Artists Equity Association Newsletter, Philadelphia Chapter*, Vol. 2, No. 1 (July 1954), with permission of the Keene family.

The Altered Ego: Paul Keene Abroad

Plans for LaSalle University Art Museum's exhibition, *Paul Keene: Post-War Explorations in Painting*, began with the discovery of paintings stored in the attic of the Keene home. Hidden away for decades, these works are a rich record of Paul Keene's early career. His G.I. Bill opportunity to work in Paris (1949-1951) was soon followed by a John Hay Whitney Fellowship which supported a two-year artist-in-residency at the Centre d'Arte, Port-au-Prince, Haiti (1952-1954).

Early educational art training in Philadelphia prepared him for these life-changing opportunities. As a teenager Paul began Saturday morning drawing classes at Philadelphia's Fleisher Art Memorial. He majored in art and, after graduating from Central High School, enrolled at what is now University of the Arts in Philadelphia. There Paul found a mentor in Robert Riggs, and he credits Riggs with steering him toward fine art and painting rather than illustration. He made etchings and relief prints for the National Youth Administration, a division of the WPA, with Herbert Pullinger leading the print making workshop. Paul began exhibiting at the Pyramid Club from its first exhibition in 1941, and around the same time at Philadelphia's Dubin Gallery.

When the United States entered World War II, Paul enlisted in the Signal Corps, a strategic move to avoid the low level jobs such as quartermaster and cook, work generally assigned to drafted African Americans. While serving in the poor conditions allotted to black soldiers in Missouri, he left base without permission to take an exam for the newly created Air Corps at Tuskegee. Paul was selected for and enjoyed the Air Corps work; he was promoted to bombardier navigator but did not see combat. After the war, he entered Temple University's Tyler School of Art at the suggestion of Riggs. At Tyler, Paul began to see the possibilities of a better life. He met sculpture student James E. Lewis, who went on to establish the art department at Morgan State University and to found the art museum there that bears his name. Lewis and his wife Jacqueline remained life-long friends of the Keene family. Tyler art historian Dr. Herman Gundersheimer and sculptor Boris Blai, both European immigrants, recognized Paul's artistic potential and helped him simultaneously earn two bachelor's degrees while working toward his master's degree by crediting his pre-war studies.

Paul and wife, Laura, left for Paris in August 1949. They met artist Sanford Greenberg and his wife Inez on the crossing, and during their second year in France they rented a house with the Greenbergs in the Paris suburb of Soisy-sous-Montmorency. The G.I. Bill allowed the Keenes to be immersed in the culture of rapidly changing post-war Paris. Paul soon met sculptor Bob Rosenwald, who was looking to turn his storefront studio into an art gallery. Bob Kulick and Bill Rivers joined in to start Gallery Huit. Paul met and befriended Stanley William Hayter, Romare Bearden, Sam Francis, Shinkichi Tajiri, Oscar Chelimsky and others at Gallery Huit. Paul also exhibited with Picasso and Léger in the Salon de Mai, and the Salon D'Hiver XLII Exposition in Paris, in addition to Galerie Huit. The Keenes' son Jacques was born in 1951 in Soisy-sous-Montmorency.

The Keenes returned to Philadelphia for only six months before Paul secured a John Hay Whitney Fellowship to work in Port-au-Prince, Haiti. His first wish was to work in Nigeria but a visa could not be had due to political turmoil. DeWitt Peters, artist and director of the Centre d'Art in Port-au-Prince, welcomed Paul, Laura and their son Jacques. Paul soon set up a studio where he directed informal classes for local artists outside of Haiti's academic system. Paul's goal for his Fellowship was to experience authentic African culture, particularly music. In Haiti he could absorb the percussive music, dance, and spiritual traditions with their strong connection to Africa. Evenings were spent with DeWitt Peters touring the countryside and observing ritual Voodoo practices, dance and music. While in Haiti, Paul exhibited with Haitian artist Antonio Joseph and encouraged George Liautaud to make his first secular sculptural works. American sculptor Jason Seeley was also an artist-in-residence at the Centre d'Art and remained a friend of the Keenes. Joseph later got together with the Keenes while visiting the United States on a Guggenheim Fellowship.

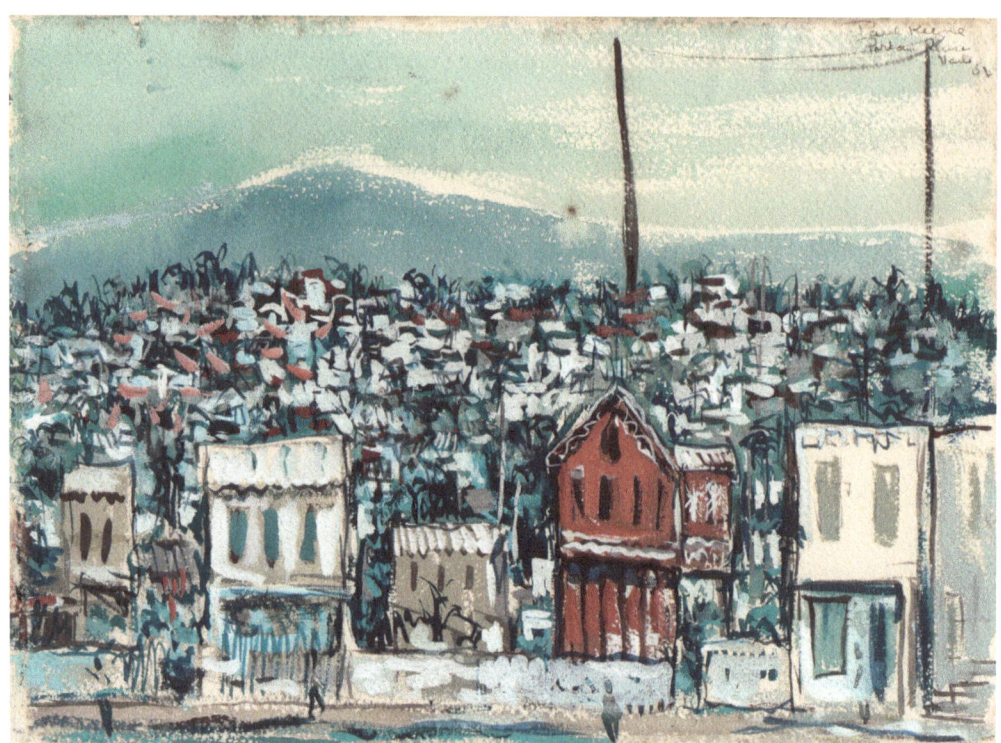

Fig. 13, Paul F. Keene, Jr. (1920-2009), *Houses, Port au Prince*, 1952, Watercolor on Paper, 10 x 14 ⅛ in., Private Collection, Courtesy of Dolan/Maxwell. Artwork © 2017 Estate of Paul F. Keene, Jr.

Paul's work met with great success after Paris and Haiti. Exhibitions at Philadelphia's Dubin Gallery upon his return from each sojourn sold out thanks to the astute Philadelphia collector and philanthropist, Benjamin Bernstein. Paintings were acquired by John Hay Whitney and Joseph Hirshhorn, and Paul was invited to exhibit at the Carlen Gallery, where Horace Pippin's paintings became part of the American art cannon.

Paul's teaching career began in earnest when he was hired by the University of the Arts in 1956. Paul and his wife Laura have explained and defined their lives from the perspective of their friendships. My own introduction to this happy couple came at the insistence of mutual friend, Anne Kaplan. Most of the work we have done together these 16 years has pretty much happened with Anne, Paul and Laura sitting around the Keenes' dining table. Selma Bortnick and Larry Day were among many life-long friendships made at Tyler and continuing later as teaching colleagues. Paul's students included Sidney Goodman, and his faculty friends included Franz Kline, Mitzi Melnicoff, Benton Spruance, Ruth Fine, Larry Day, and Anne's husband, print maker Jerome Kaplan. Paul exhibited at Terry Dintenfas's gallery in Atlantic City,

NJ, and close friendships evolved between these families, which by 1961 included the Keenes' daughter Lydia. Gladys Meyer smiles warmly while discussing Paul and the other artists she exhibited (including Day, Kaplan, David Pease, Natalie Charkow, Jimmy Lueders, Rudy Staffel and Sam Maitin) at her important Gallery 1015 in Wyncote, PA from 1958 to 1972.

This exhibition celebrates a too-little known period of Paul's career. Curators have noted that Paul arrived at abstraction about the same time as Norman Lewis and Charles Alston. The paintings are hybrids of Paul's exposure to the early Modern and Contemporary art he found in Paris and the authentic West African cultural traditions he sought in Haiti. La Salle University Art Museum, holding two large 1950s paintings donated by Bernstein, is the perfect venue to organize this exhibition, which will travel to the Georgia College Museum of Fine Arts and the North Carolina Central University Art Museum.

Ron Rumford
Artist and Director, Dolan/Maxwell

Paul Keene: Post-War Explorations in Painting

Catalogue of Artworks

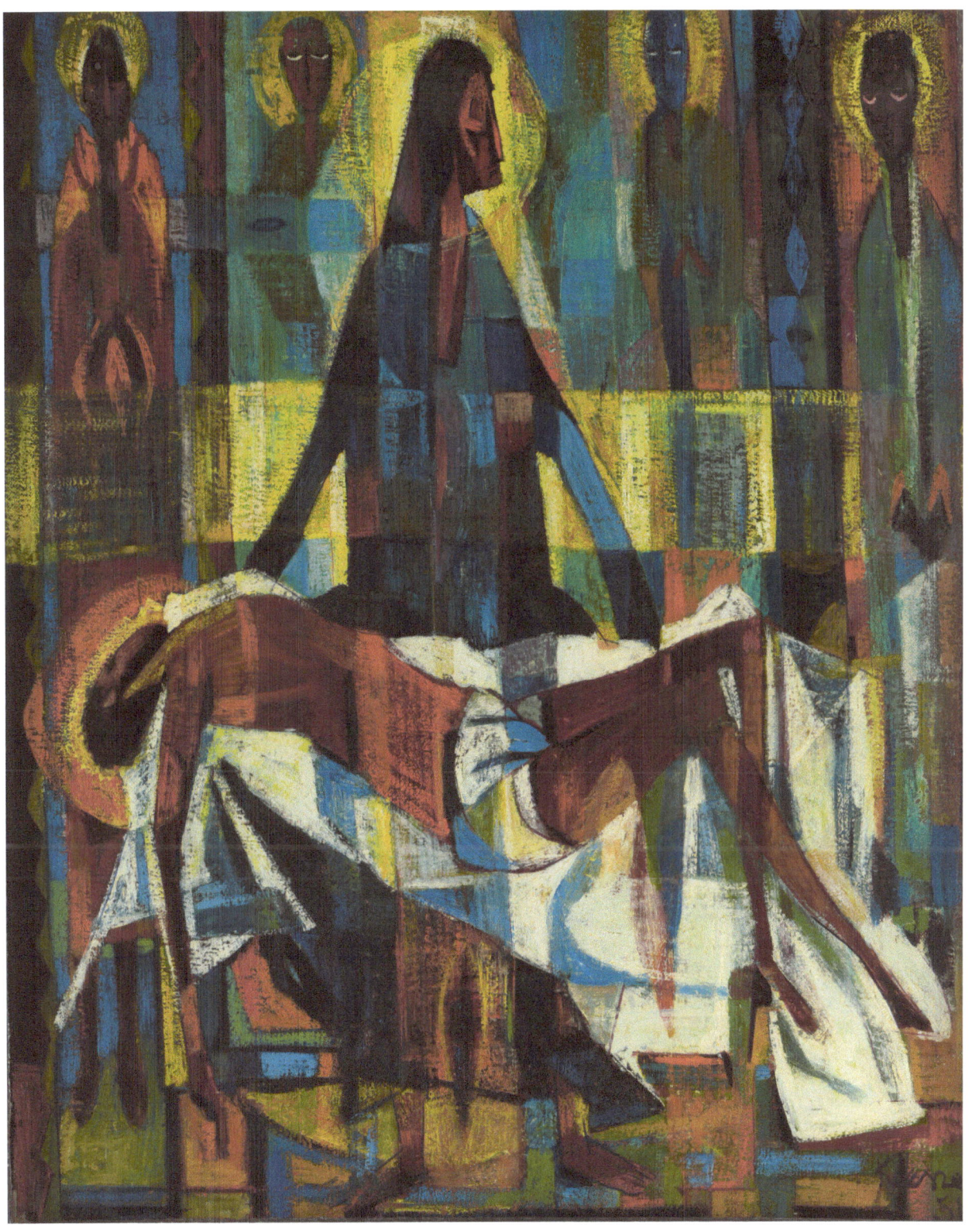

Cat. 1, Paul F. Keene, Jr. (1920-2009), *Pietà, Soisy*, 1951, Oil on Board, 20 x 16 in., Courtesy of the Keene Family and Dolan/Maxwell. Artwork © 2017 Estate of Paul F. Keene, Jr.

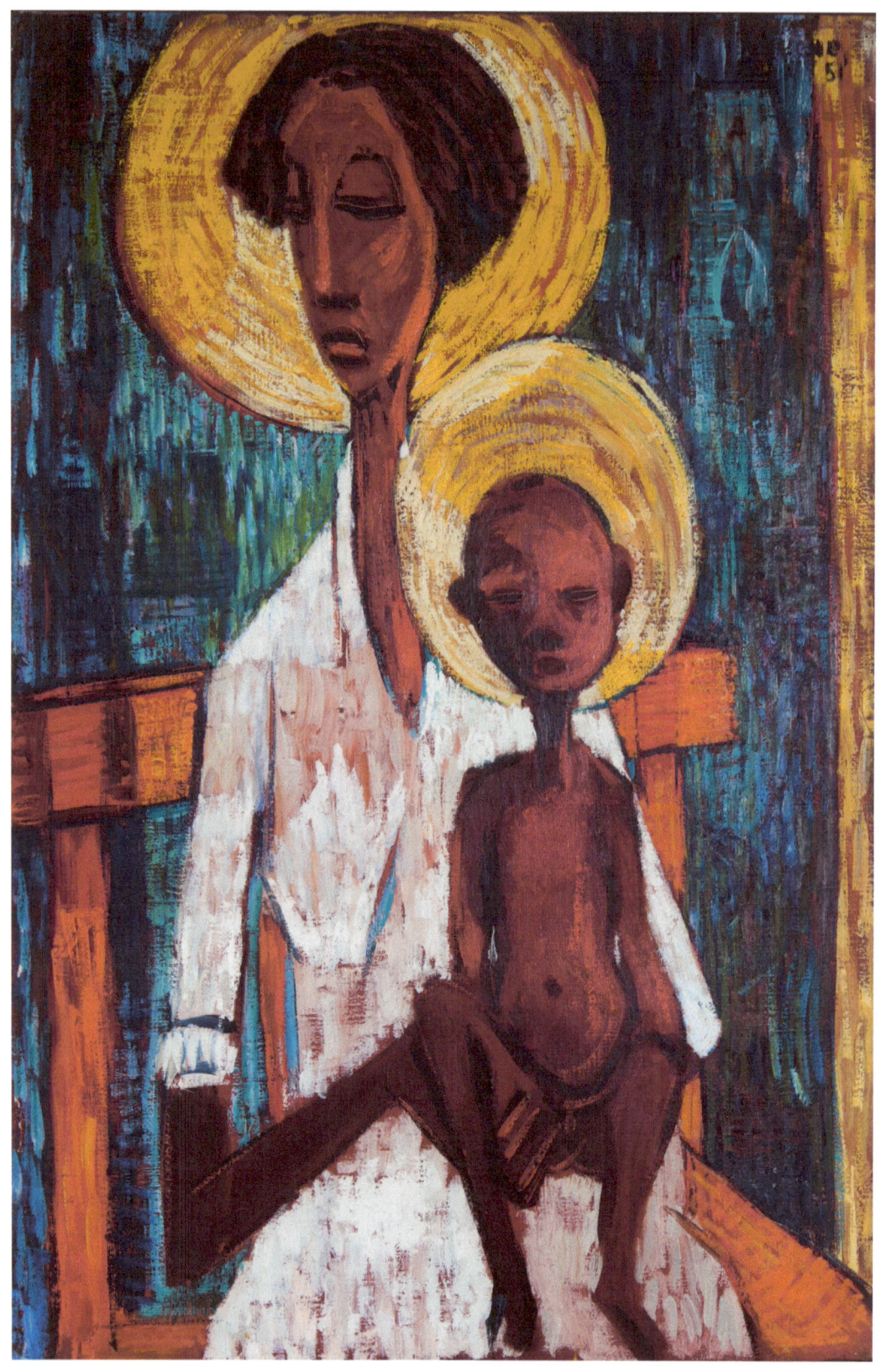

Cat. 2, Paul F. Keene, Jr. (1920-2009), *Mother and Son*, 1951, Oil on Canvas, 32 x 21 in., Private Collection. Artwork ©
2017 Estate of Paul F. Keene, Jr.

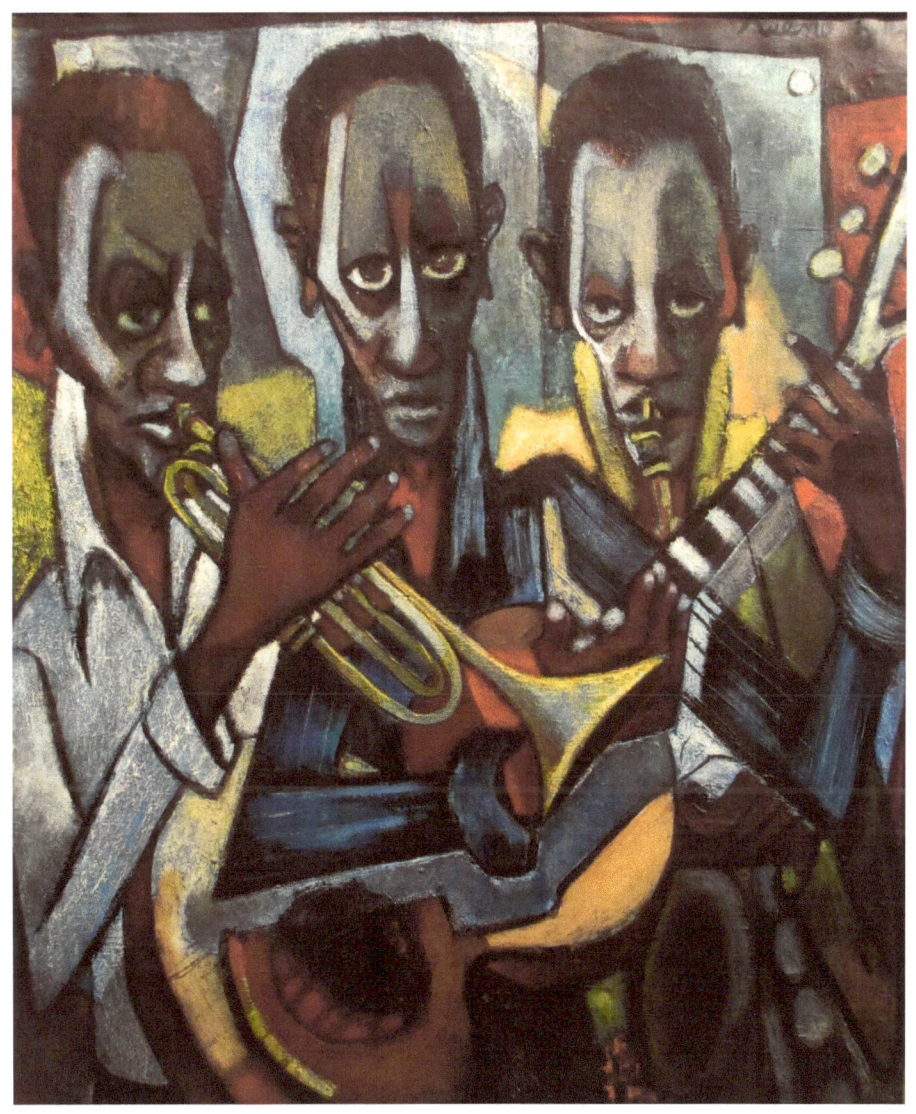

Cat. 3, Paul F. Keene, Jr. (1920-2009), *Symphony in Blue*, 1951, Oil on Canvas, 29 ½ x 25 in., Artwork from Villanova University Collection, Gift of Benjamin D. Bernstein. Artwork © 2017 Estate of Paul F. Keene, Jr.

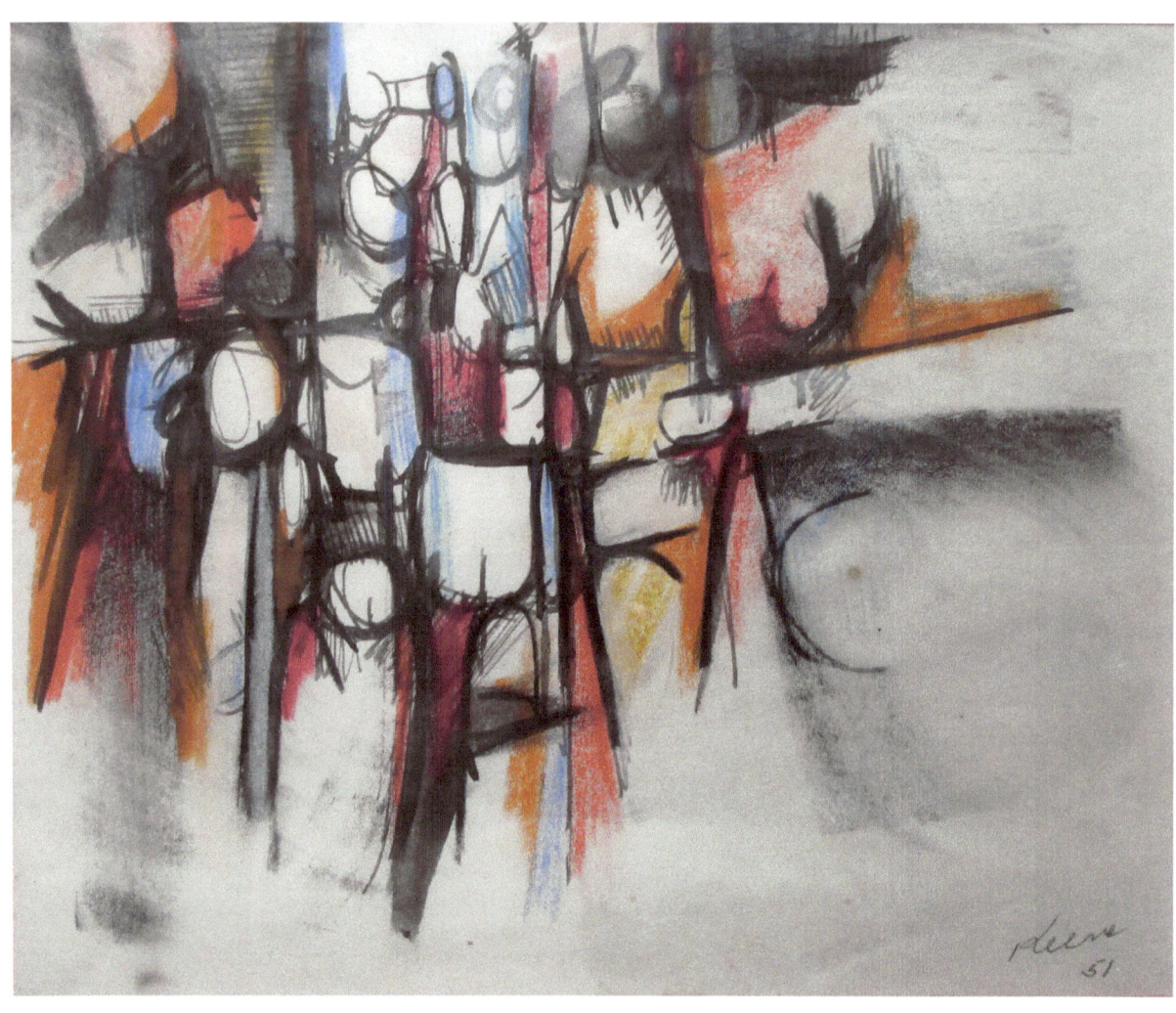

Cat. 4, Paul F. Keene, Jr. (1920-2009), *Untitled Abstract*, 1951, Graphite and Pastel, 14 x 16 in., Collection of Lewis Tanner Moore. Artwork © 2017 Estate of Paul F. Keene, Jr.

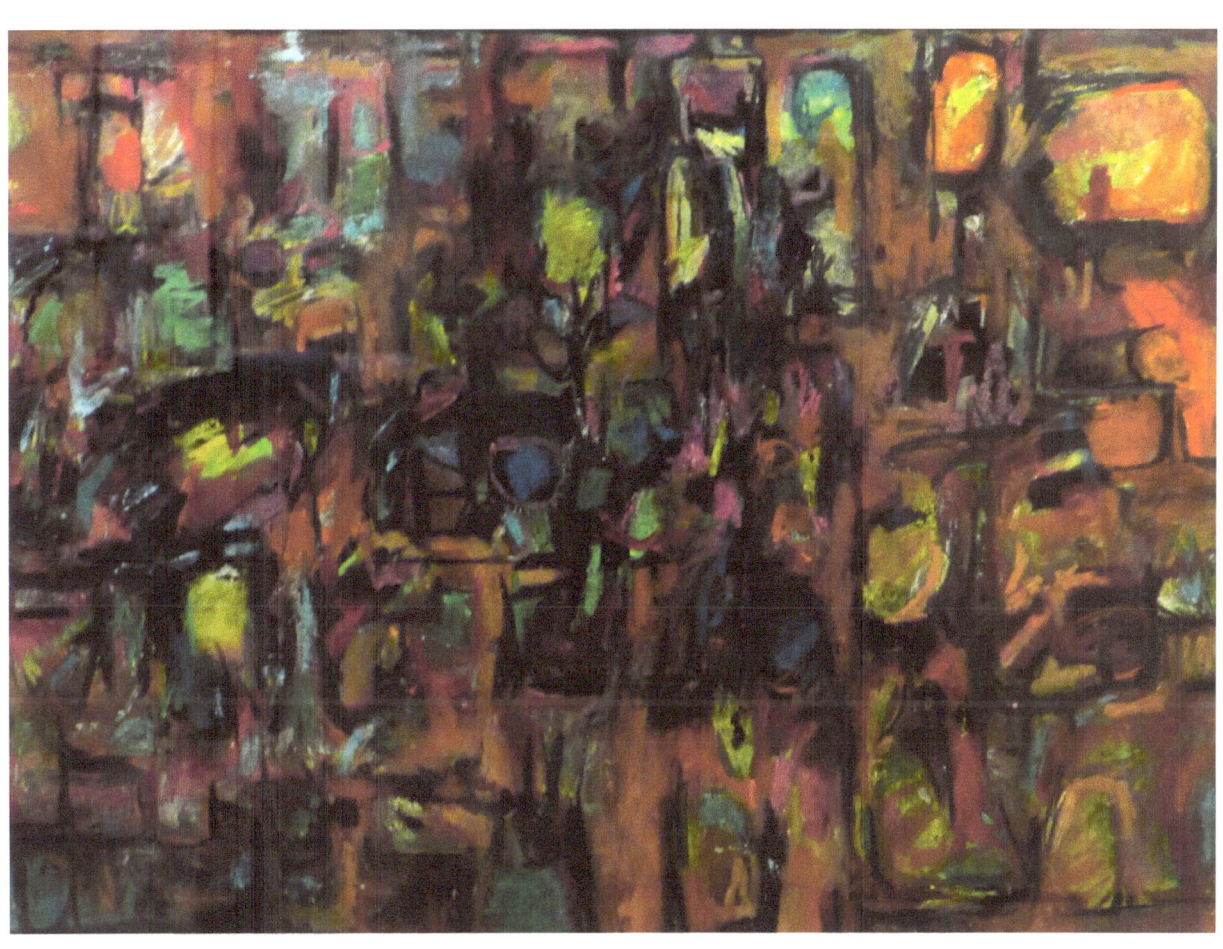

Cat. 5, Paul F. Keene, Jr. (1920-2009), *Abstract*, 1951, Oil on Paper, 22 x 30 in., Artwork from Villanova University Collection, Gift of Edward I. Bernstein. Artwork © 2017 Estate of Paul F. Keene, Jr.

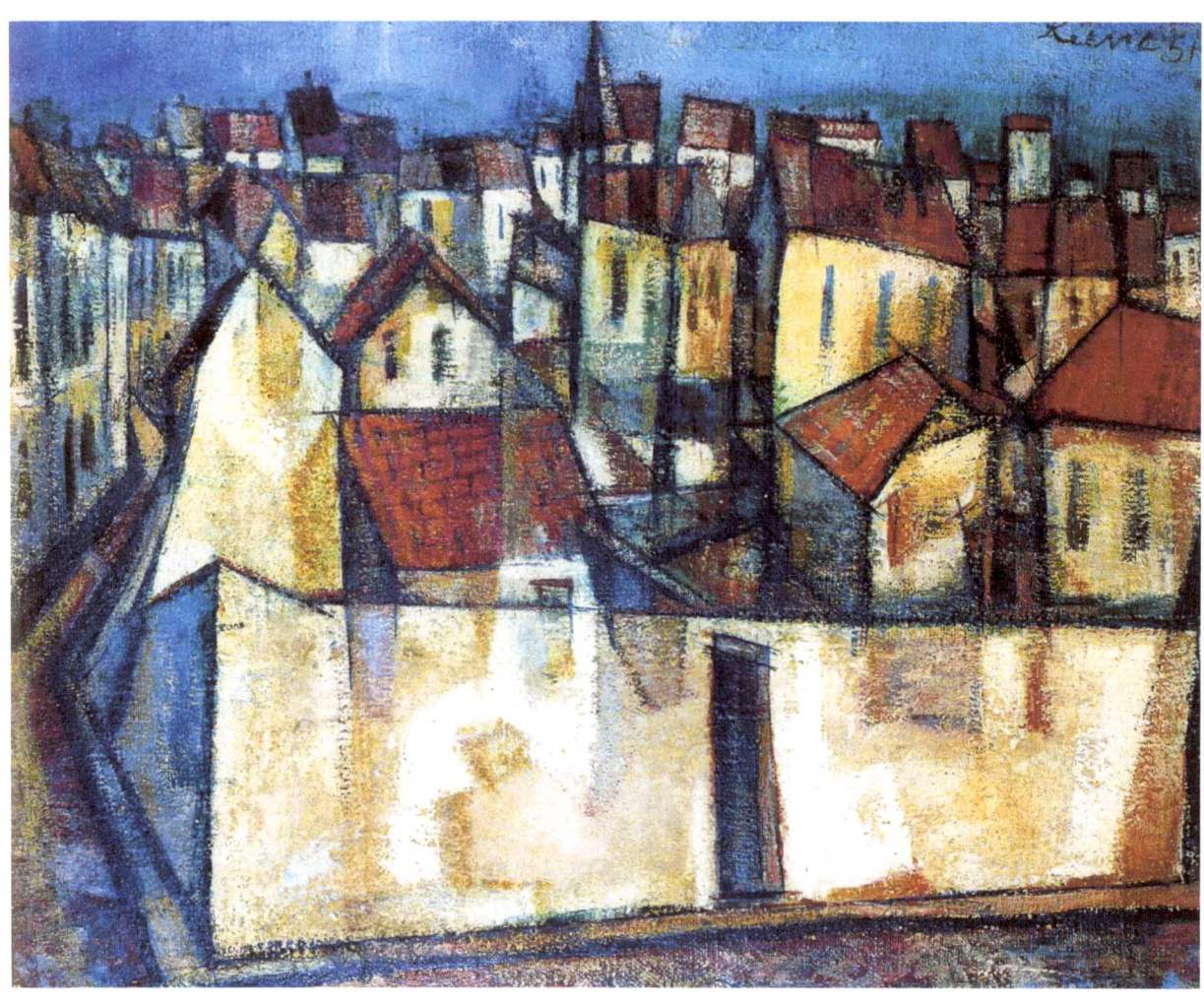

Cat. 6, Paul F. Keene, Jr. (1920-2009), *Soisy-sous-Montmorency*, 1951, Oil on Canvas, 23 x 32 in., Collection of Lewis Tanner Moore. Artwork © 2017 Estate of Paul F. Keene, Jr.

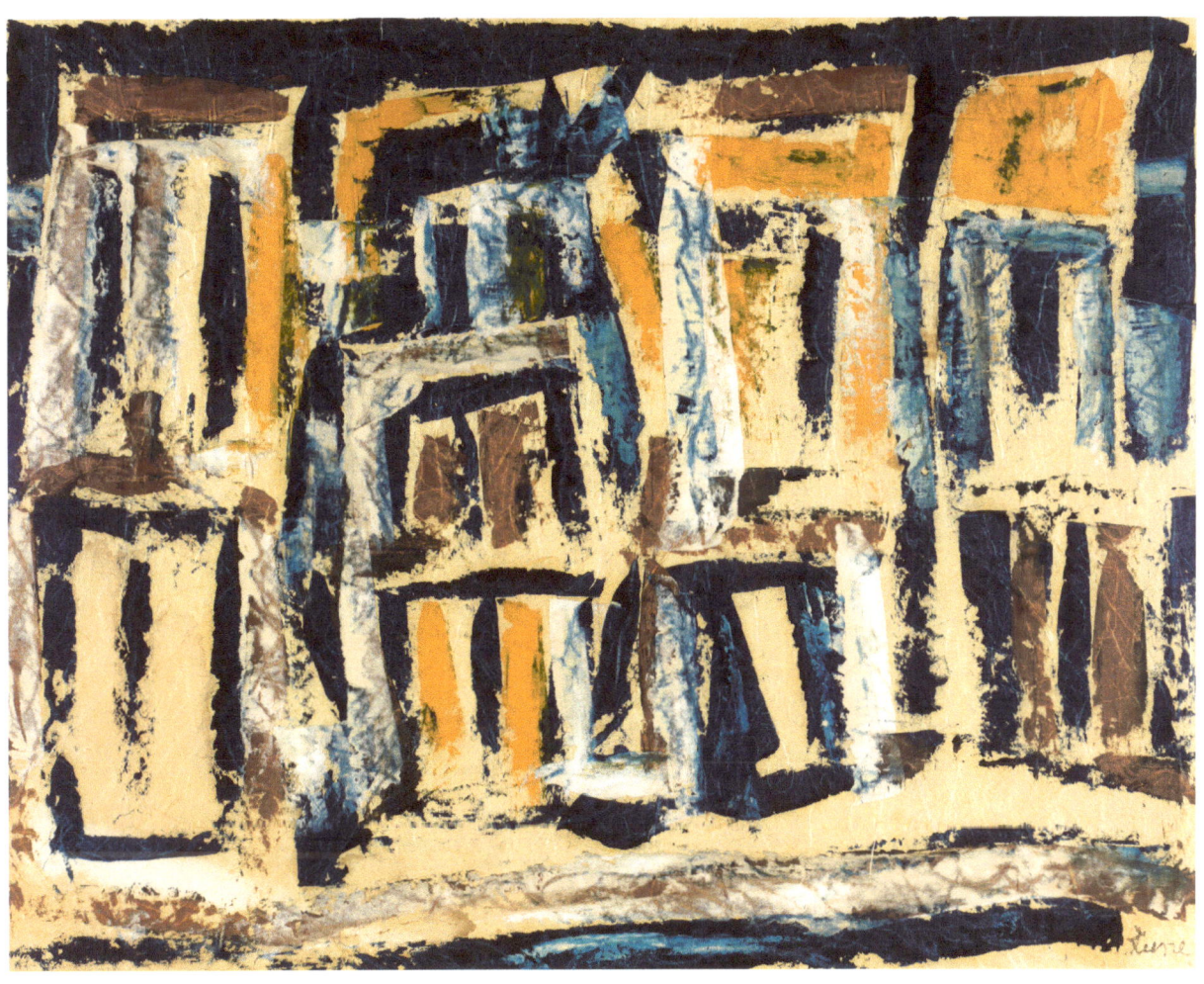

Cat. 7, Paul F. Keene, Jr. (1920-2009), *Untitled (Abstract)*, 1952, Acrylic on Rice Paper, adhered to board, 19 ¼ x 25 in., Courtesy of the Pennsylvania Academy of the Fine Arts, Philadelphia. Gift of Benjamin D. Bernstein and Robin J. Bernstein, 2002.9.13. Artwork © 2017 Estate of Paul F. Keene, Jr.

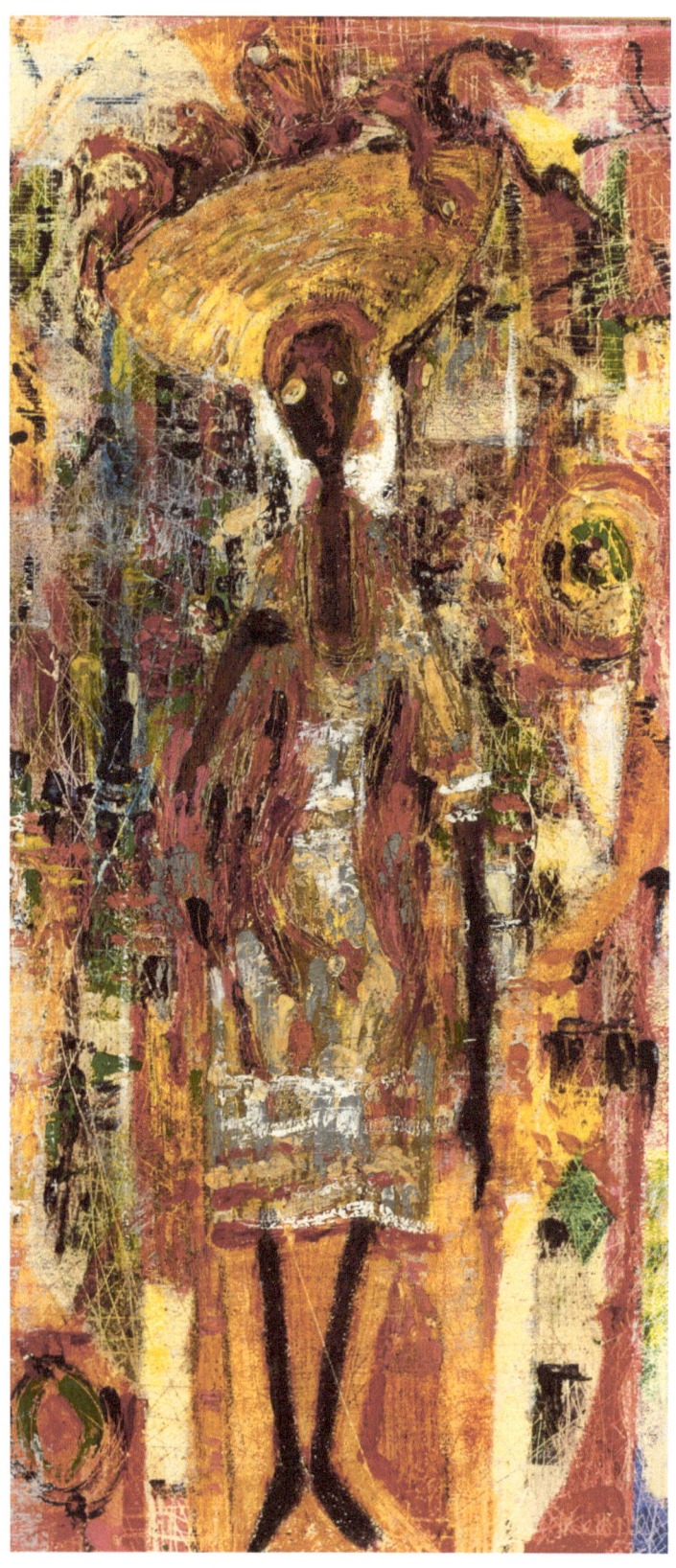

Cat. 8, Paul F. Keene, Jr. (1920-2009), *Chicken Woman*, 1953, Encaustic on Cardboard, 21 ¼ x 11 in., Courtesy of the Pennsylvania Academy of the Fine Arts, Philadelphia. Gift of Benjamin D. Bernstein, 1959.10.2. Artwork © 2017 Estate of Paul F. Keene, Jr.

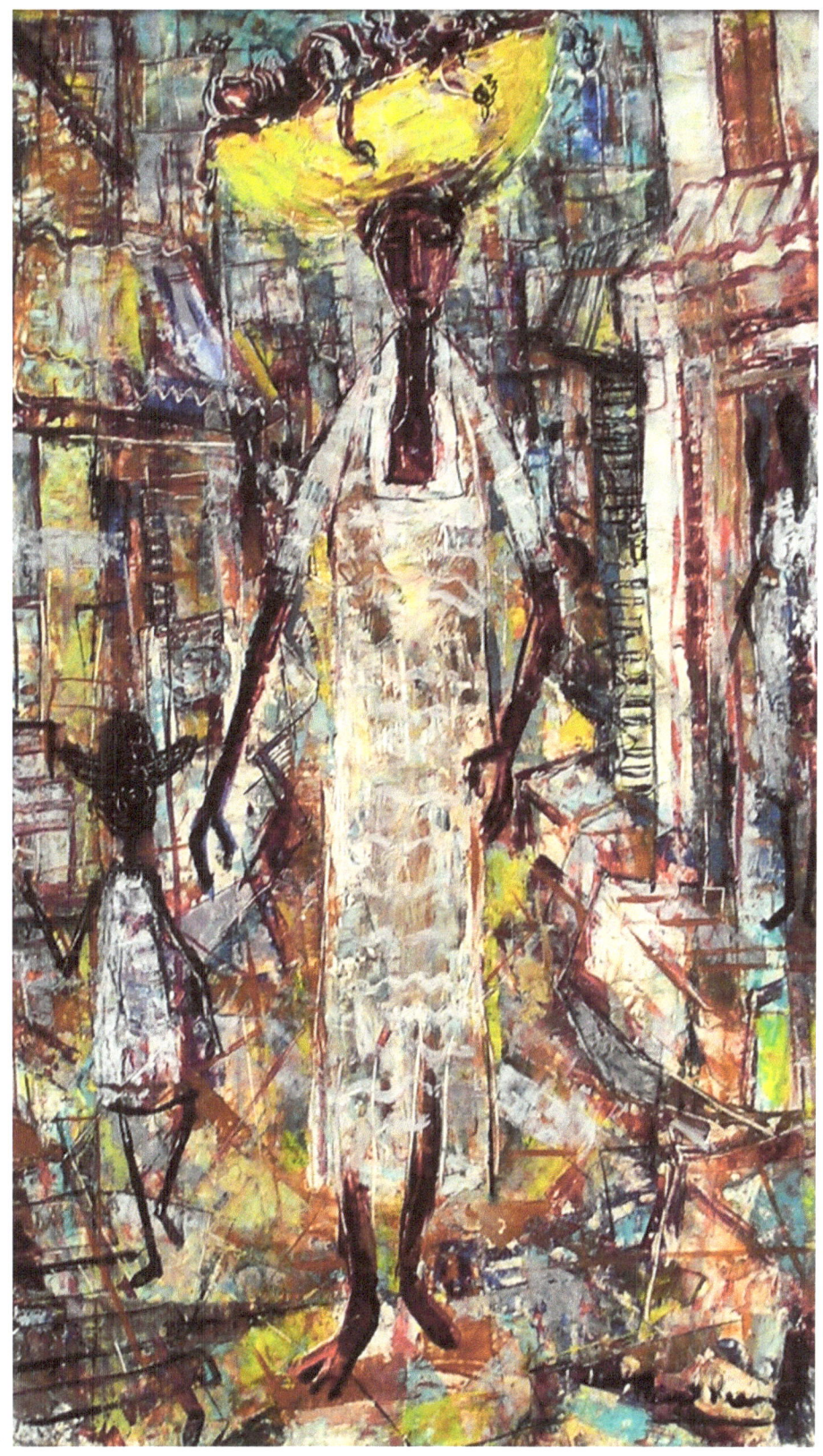

Cat. 9, Paul F. Keene, Jr. (1920-2009), *Chicken Woman and Child*, c. 1953, Oil on Canvas, 21 ⅛ x 12 ½ in., Courtesy of Gladys Meyers and Dolan/Maxwell. Artwork © 2017 Estate of Paul F. Keene, Jr.

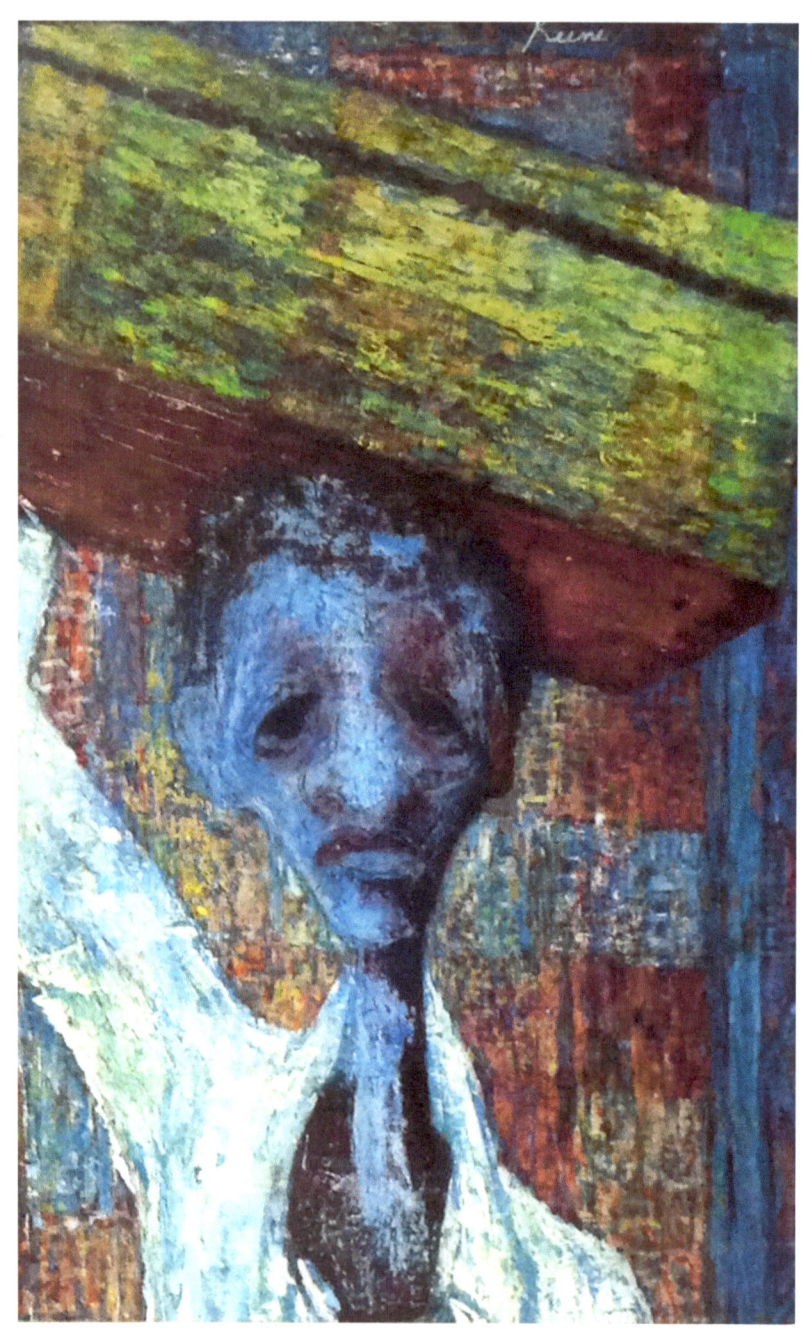

Cat. 10, Paul F. Keene, Jr. (1920-2009), *Blue Man (Carrying a Coffin)*, c. 1953, Oil on Masonite, 29 x 21 ½ in, Courtesy of Dr. William Dodd and Dolan/Maxwell. Artwork © 2017 Estate of Paul F. Keene, Jr.

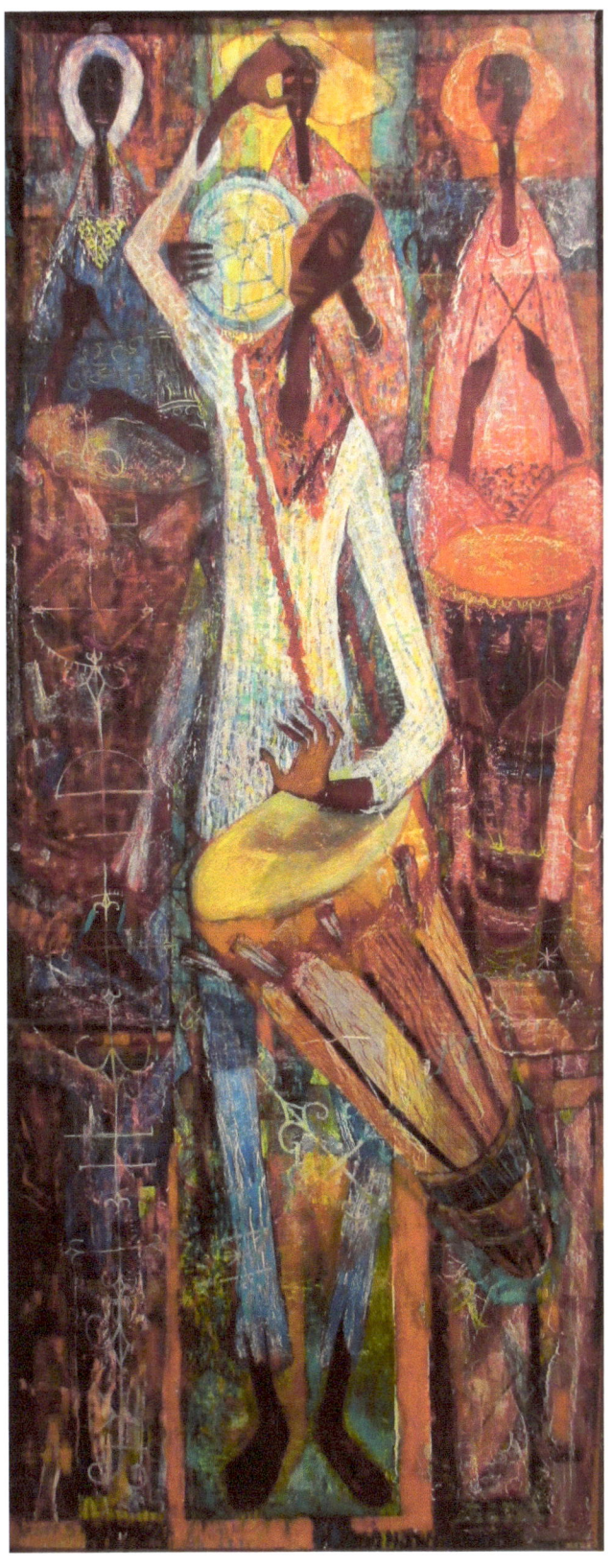

Cat. 11, Paul F. Keene, Jr. (1920-2009), *Drummer*, 1952, Oil on Masonite,
48 x 20 in., Artwork from Villanova University Collection, Gift of
Benjamin D. Bernstein. Artwork © 2017 Estate of Paul F. Keene, Jr.

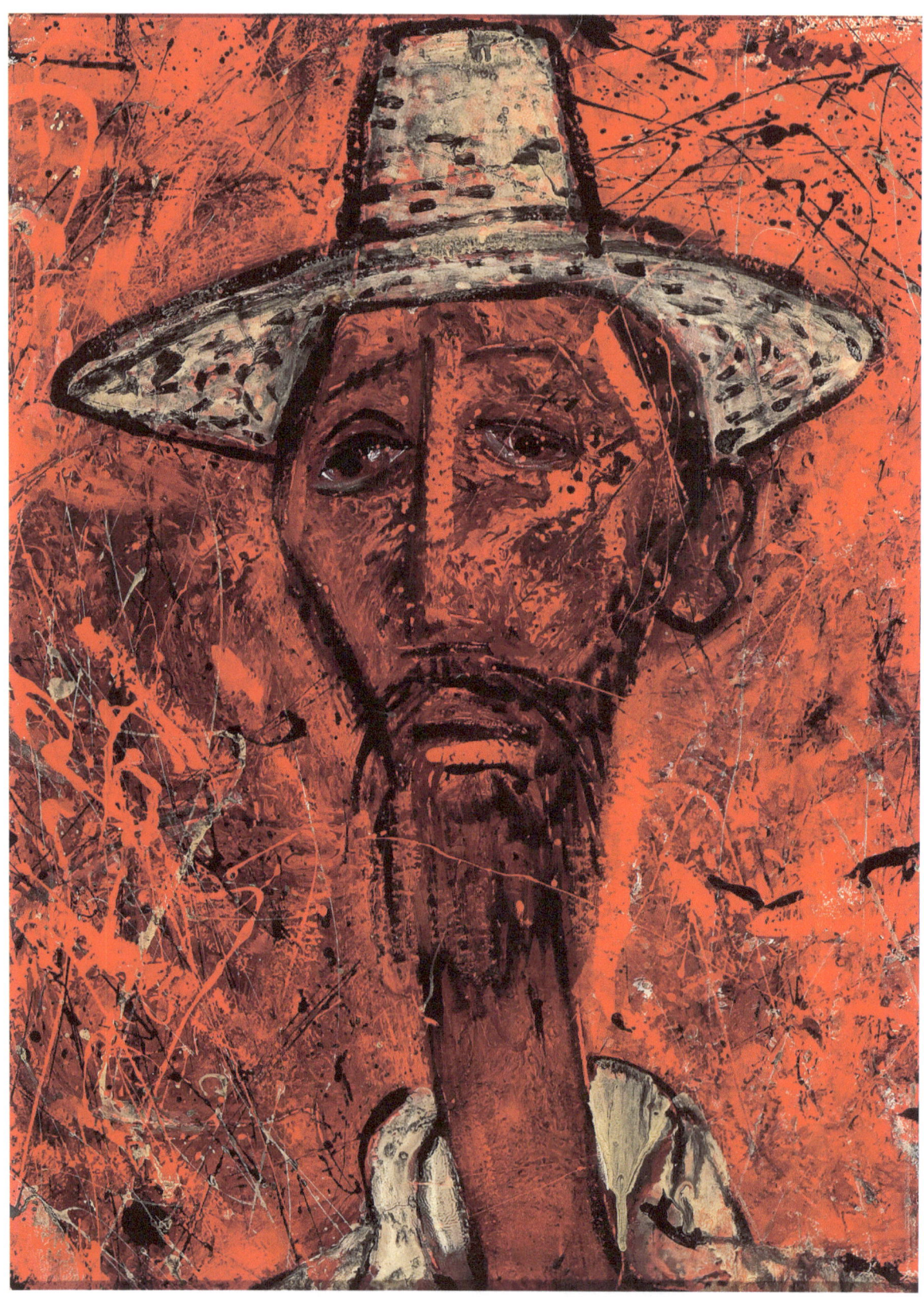

Cat. 12, Paul F. Keene, Jr. (1920-2009), *Voodoo Priest*, c. 1953, Oil on Board, 23 ½ x 17 ¾ in., Woodmere Art Museum: Gift from the collection of Benjamin D. Bernstein, 1995. Photography: Rick Echelmeyer. Artwork © 2017 Estate of Paul F. Keene, Jr.

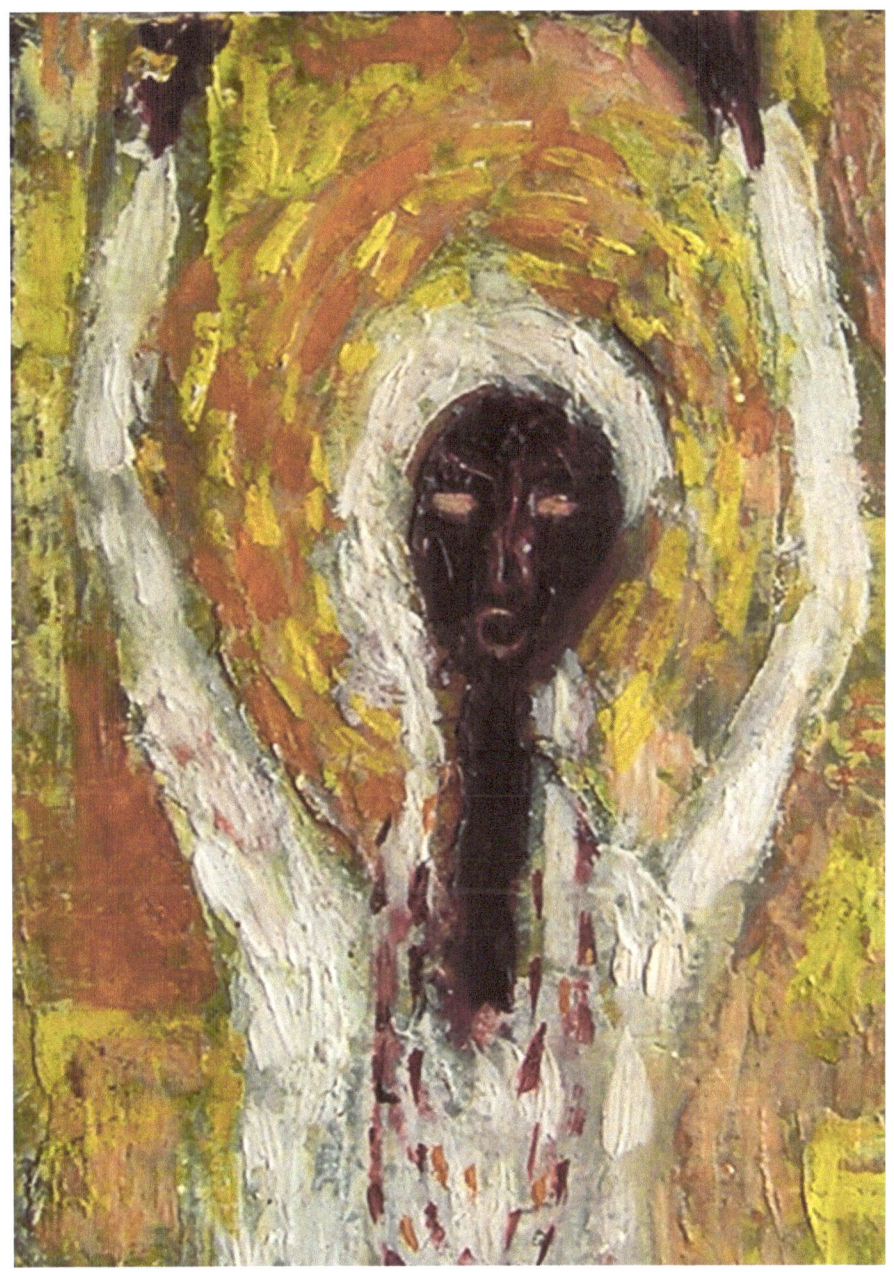

Cat. 13, Paul F. Keene, Jr. (1920-2009), *Arms Up*, c. 1952, Oil on Board, 5 ¾ x 4 in., Courtesy of Dr. William Dodd and Dolan/Maxwell. Artwork © 2017 Estate of Paul F. Keene, Jr.

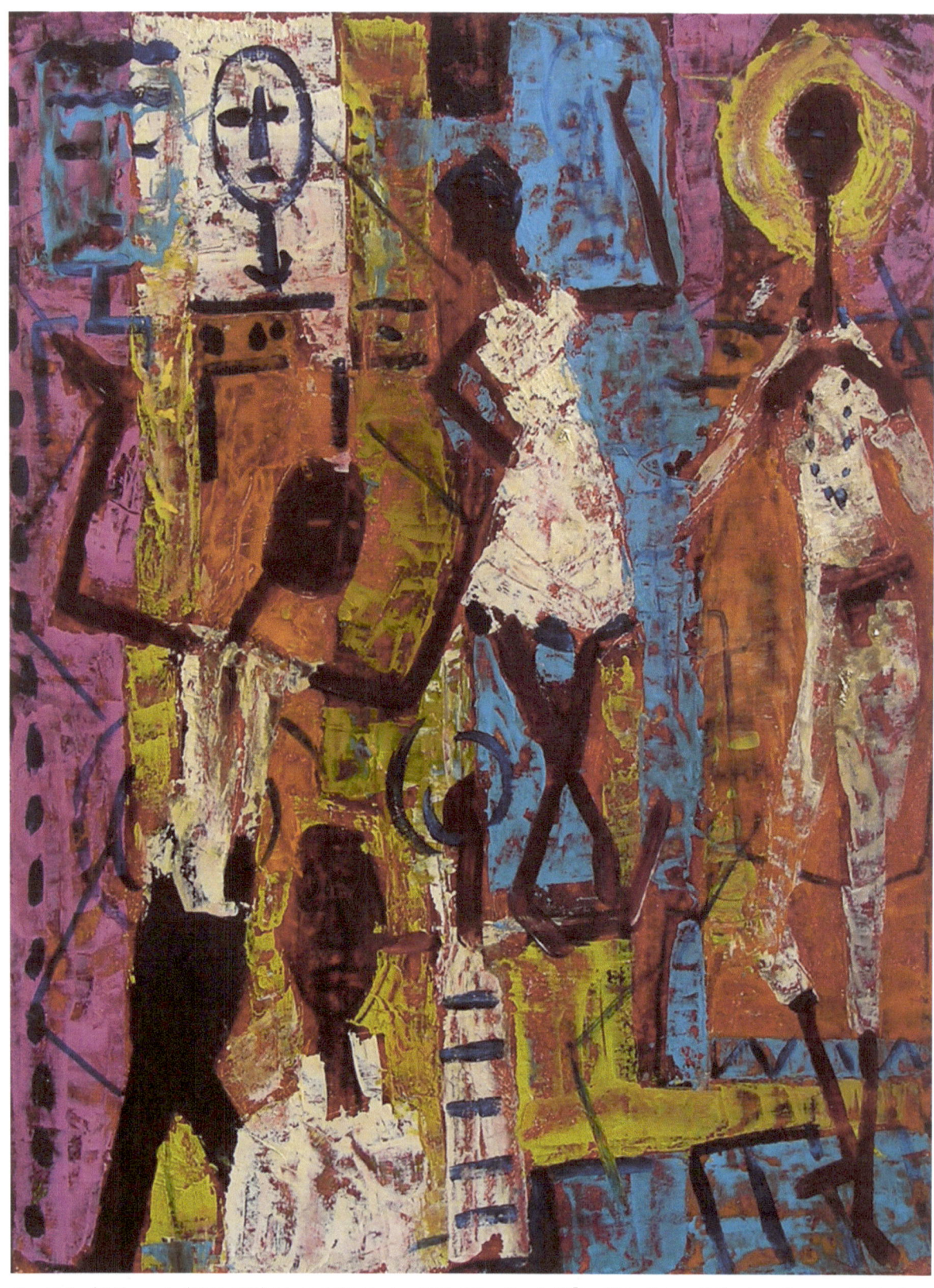

Cat. 14, Paul F. Keene, Jr. (1920-2009), *Untitled (Haitian)*, c. 1952, Oil on Panel, 15 ⅞ x 12 in, Private Collection, Courtesy of Dolan/ Maxwell. Artwork © 2017 Estate of Paul F. Keene, Jr.

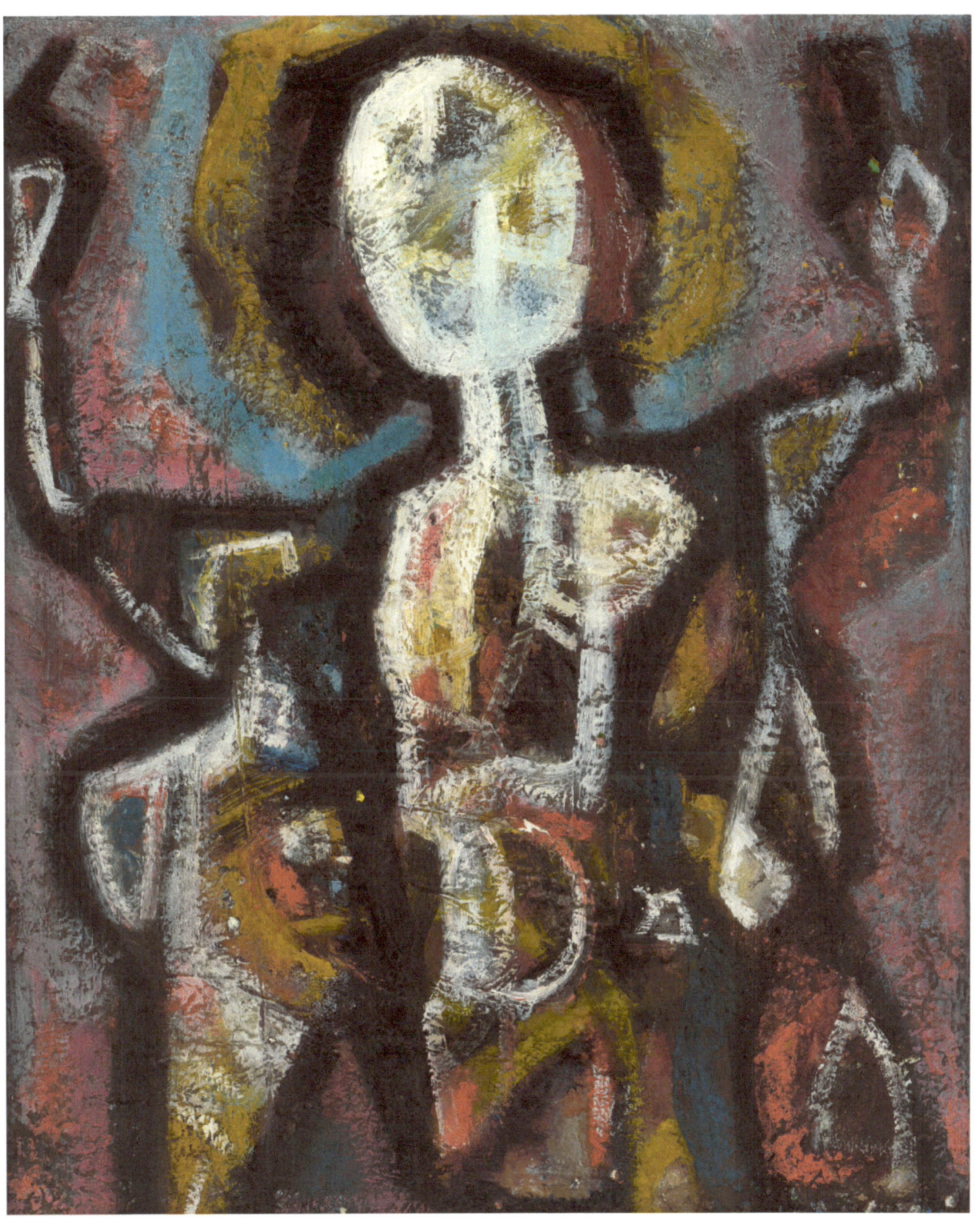

Cat. 15, Paul F. Keene, Jr. (1920-2009), *Figure, Haiti*, c. 1952, Oil on Board, 25 ⅝ x 21 ¼ in., Courtesy of the Keene Family and Dolan/Maxwell. Artwork © 2017 Estate of Paul F. Keene, Jr.

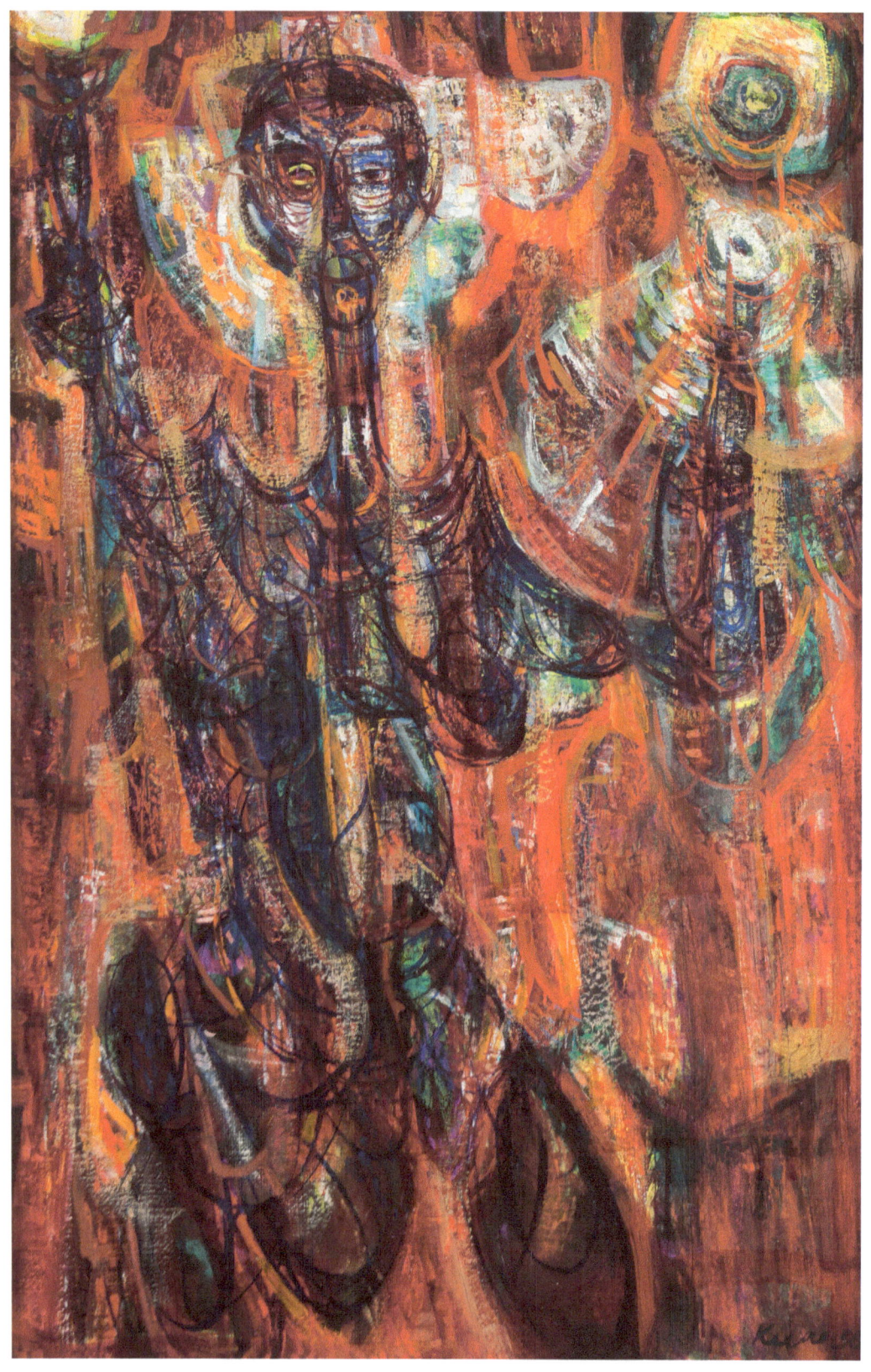

Cat. 16, Paul F. Keene, Jr. (1920-2009), *The Sorceress*, 1956, Oil on Canvas, 23 ¼ x 15 ¼ in., Collection of La Salle University Art Museum, Gift of Benjamin D. Bernstein, 91-P-377. Artwork © 2017 Estate of Paul F. Keene, Jr. and La Salle University Art Museum.

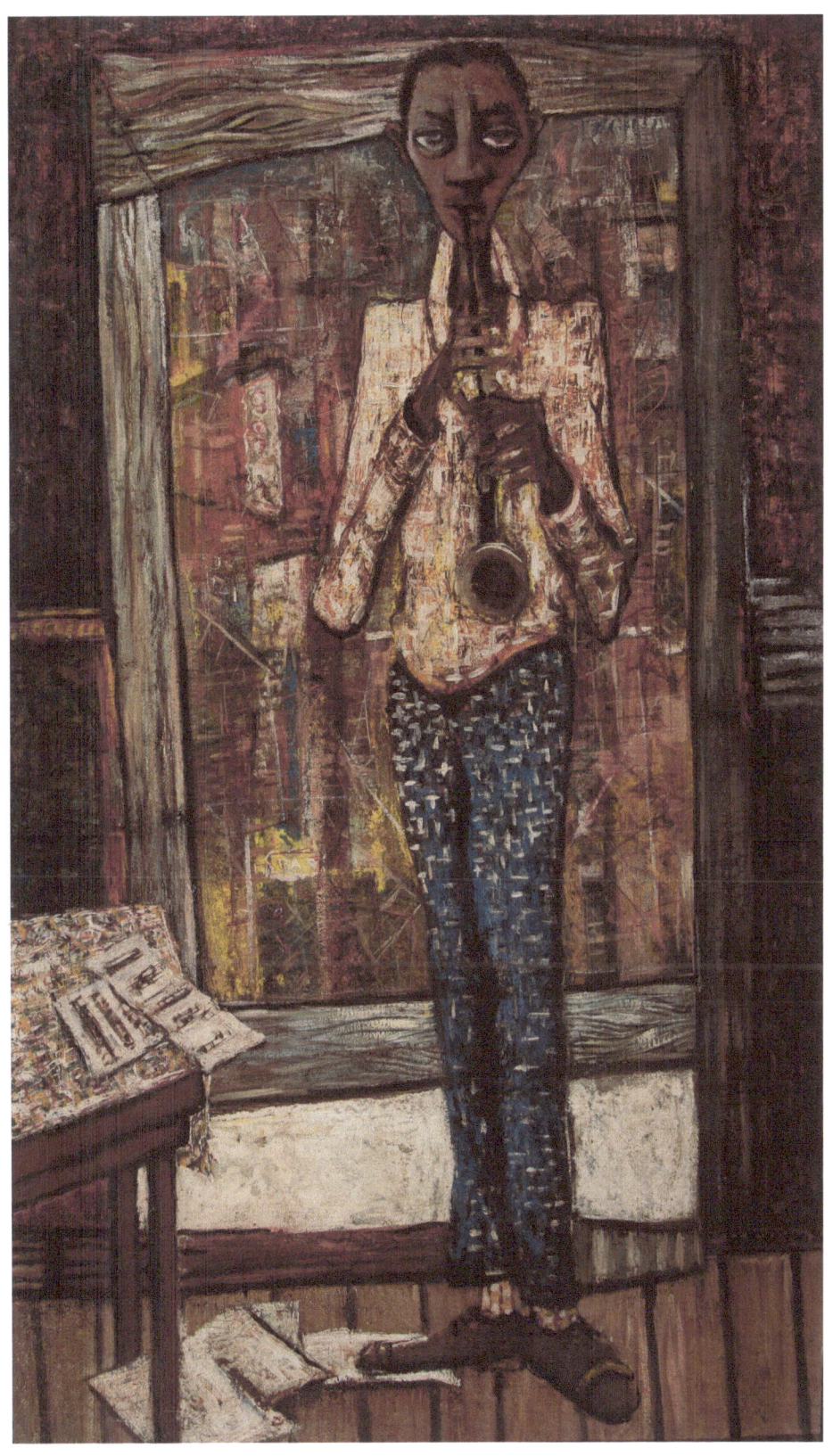

Cat. 17, Paul F. Keene, Jr. (1920-2009), *Clarinet Player*, c. 1955, Oil on Masonite, 41 ½ x 24 ½ in., Courtesy of the African American Museum in Philadelphia. Artwork © 2017 Estate of Paul F. Keene, Jr.

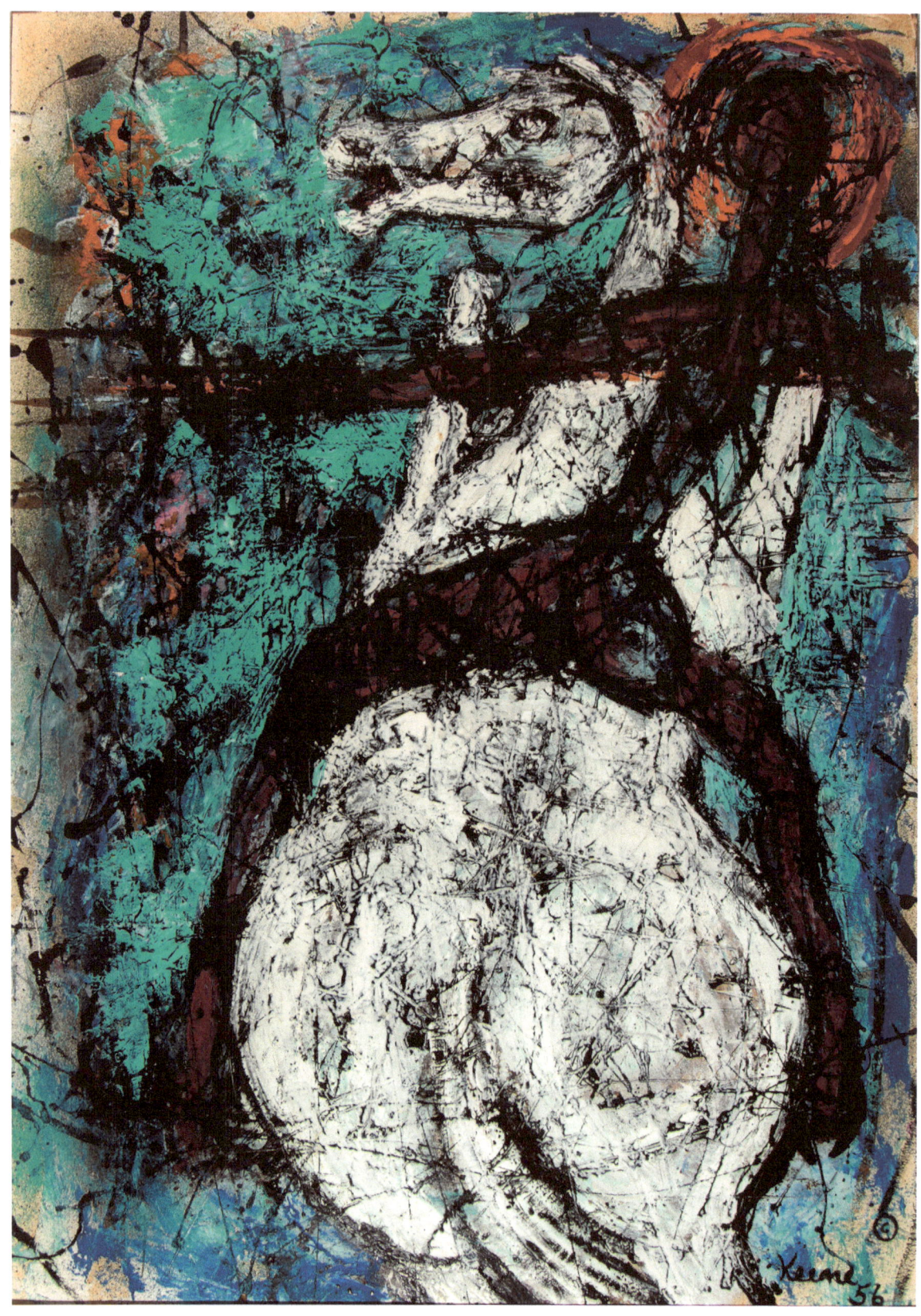

Cat. 18, Paul F. Keene, Jr. (1920-2009), *Horseman of the Apocalypse*, 1956, Oil on Artist Board, 30 x 22 in., Collection of Lewis Tanner Moore. Artwork © 2017 Estate of Paul F. Keene, Jr.

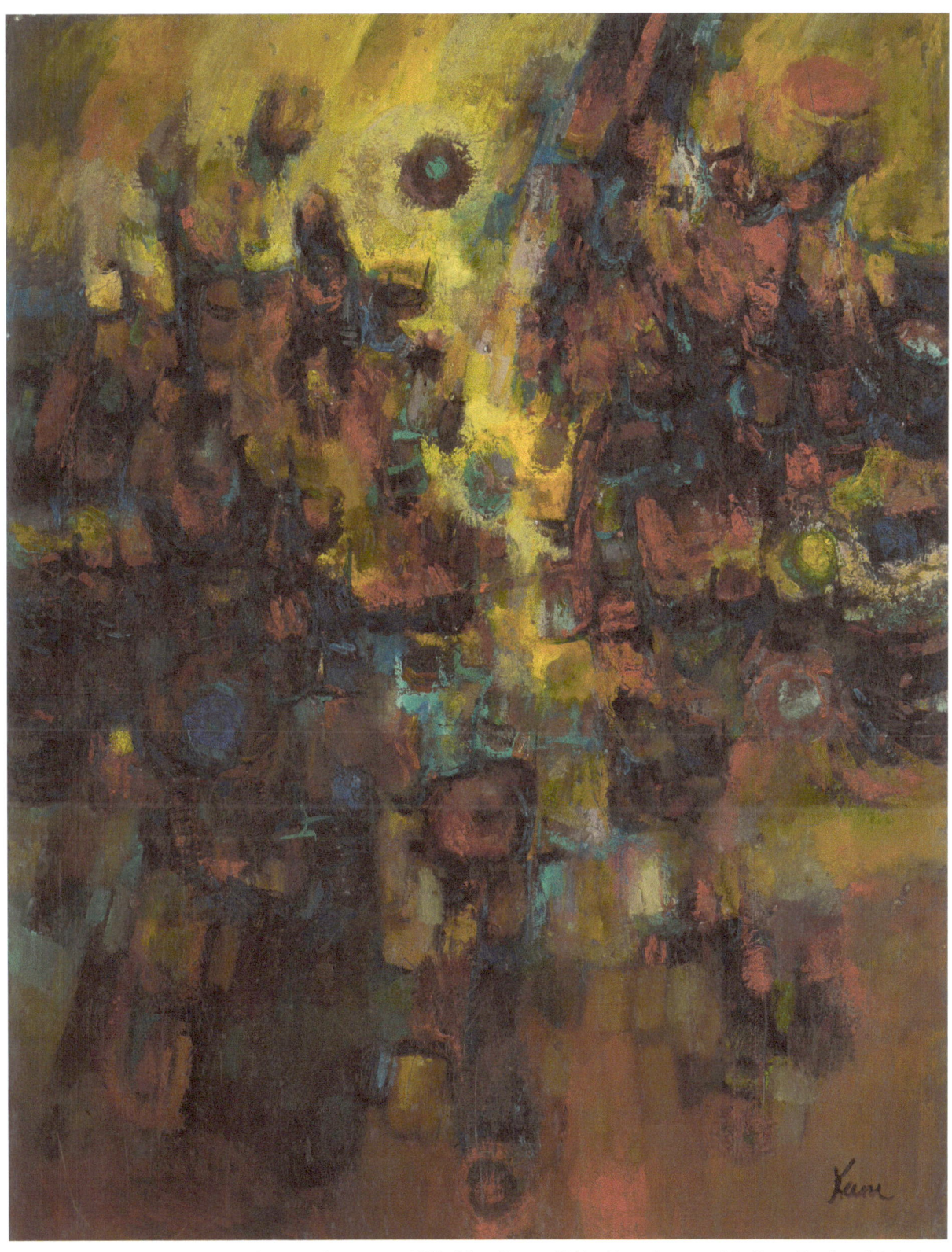

Cat. 19, Paul F. Keene, Jr. (1920-2009), *Haiti Abstraction*, c. 1958, Oil on Canvas, 30 ½ x 24 in., Courtesy of the Keene Family and Dolan/
Maxwell. Artwork © 2017 Estate of Paul F. Keene, Jr.

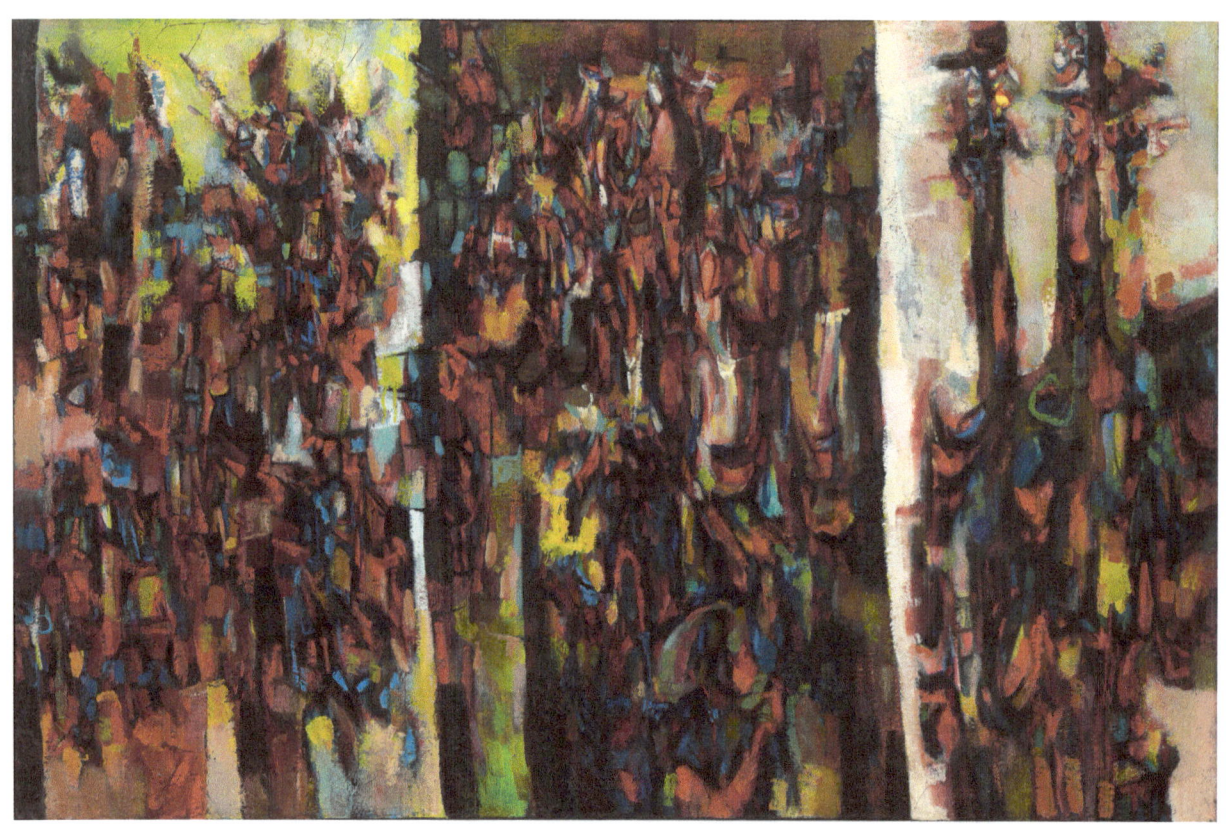

Cat. 20, Paul F. Keene, Jr. (1920-2009), *Mardi Gras Parade*, c. 1953, Oil on Canvas, 34 x 52 in., Courtesy of the Keene Family and Dolan/Maxwell. Artwork © 2017 Estate of Paul F. Keene, Jr.

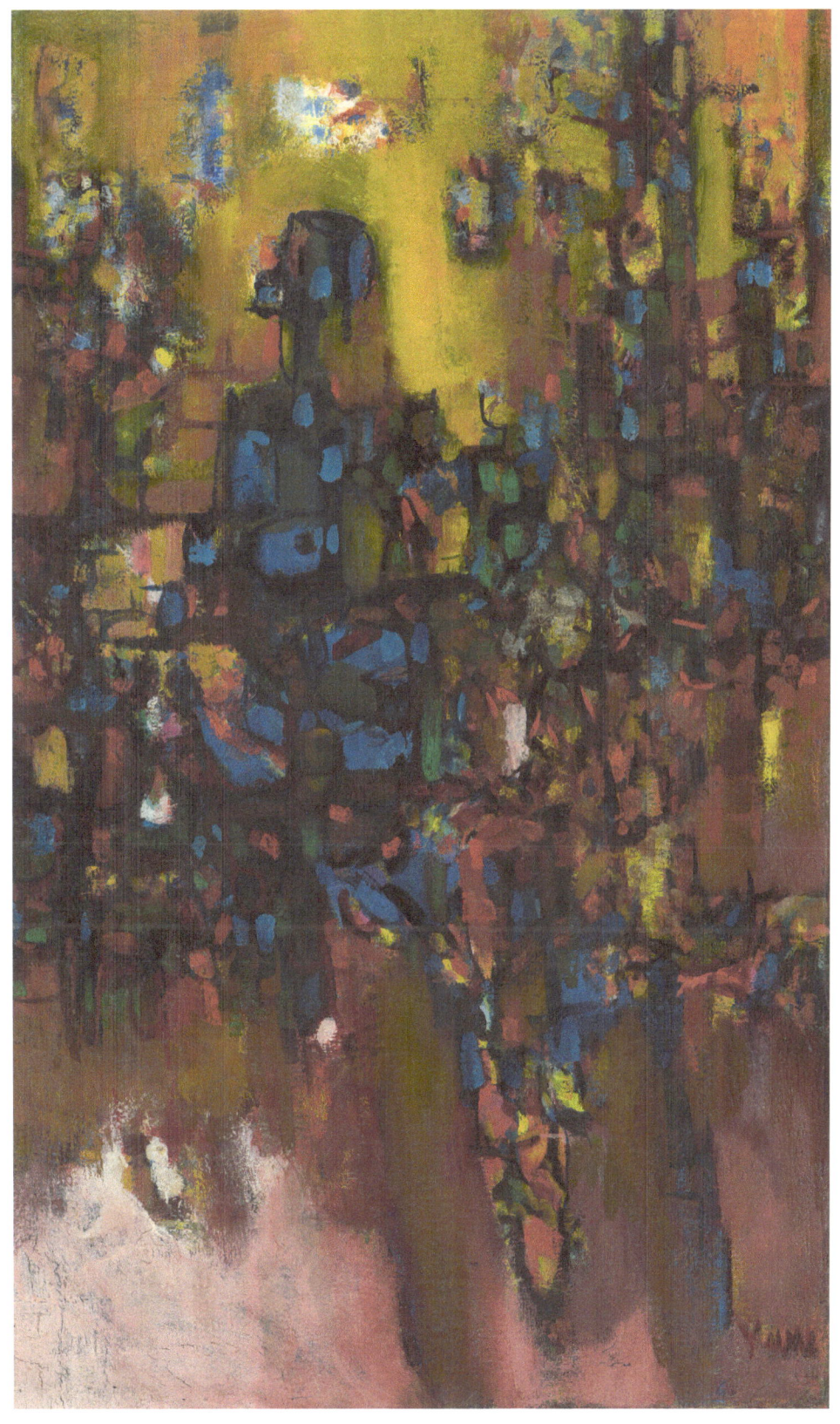

Cat. 21, Paul F. Keene, Jr. (1920-2009), *The Altered Ego*, c. 1955, Oil on Canvas, 53 x 37 ½ in., Courtesy of the Keene Family and Dolan/Maxwell. Artwork © 2017 Estate of Paul F. Keene, Jr.

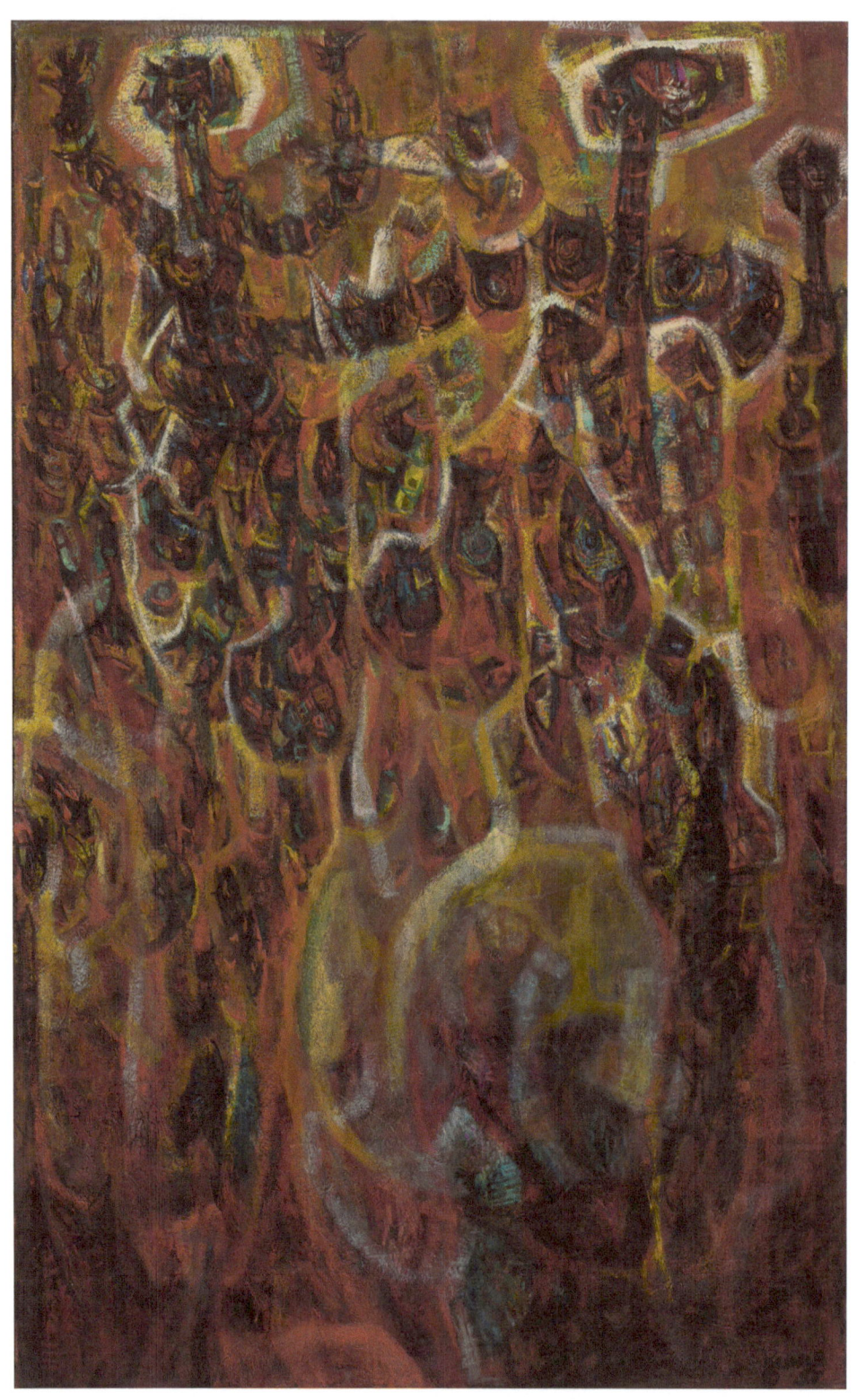

Cat. 22, Paul F. Keene, Jr. (1920-2009), *Baroque Warriors*, 1957, Oil on Canvas, 59 x 37 ½ in., Courtesy of the Keene Family and Dolan/Maxwell. Artwork © 2017 Estate of Paul F. Keene, Jr.

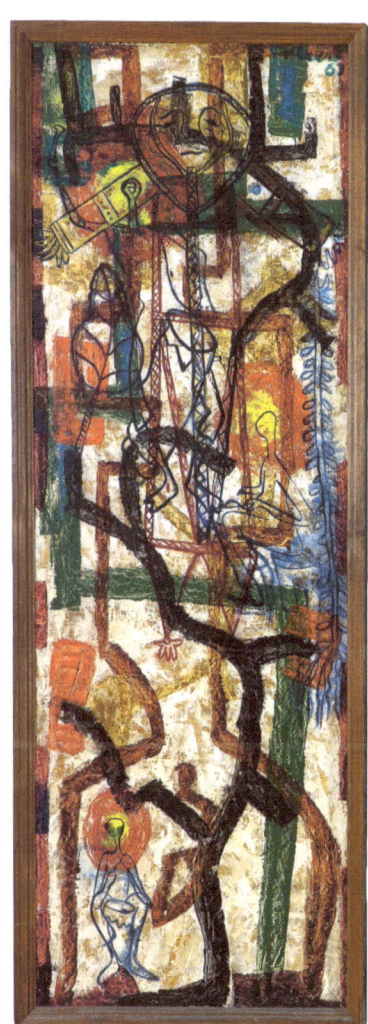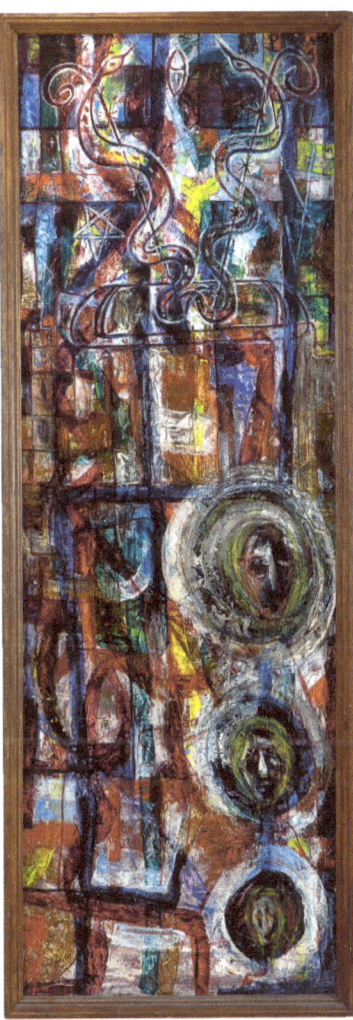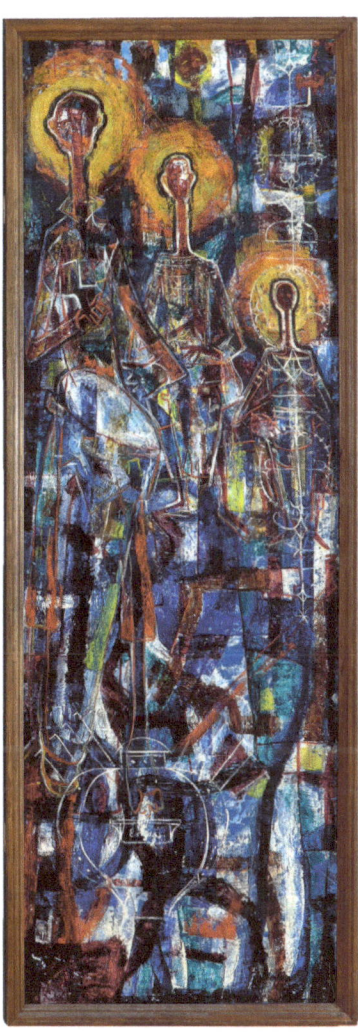

Cat. 23, Paul F. Keene, Jr. (1920-2009), *Haitian Voodoo Spirits*, 1953, Oil on Wood Panels, 69 ¼ x 80 in. (total), Collection of La Salle University Art Museum, Gift of Benjamin D. Bernstein, 01-P-474(1-3). Artwork © 2017 Estate of Paul F. Keene, Jr. and La Salle University Art Museum.

La Salle University Art Museum

The La Salle University Art Museum opened its doors in 1975 as an educational resource for La Salle students, especially those majoring in art history, as well as for the communities in the surrounding area. The Art Museum's collection had its beginnings 10 years earlier. At the University's fall Honors Convocation in 1965, John Walker, director of the National Gallery of Art in Washington, D.C., delivered the address, and well-known collector Lessing Rosenwald and American artist Andrew Wyeth received honorary degrees. On this auspicious occasion, the University announced that it was beginning a degree program in art history and had begun acquiring art. What began as a modest study collection has since blossomed into a well-established museum, now considered one of the city's cultural gems. Currently, La Salle is the only university in the Philadelphia area to own a permanent display of paintings, drawings, and sculptures from the Renaissance to the present. The collection is housed in a series of period rooms in the lower level of Olney Hall on the University's Main Campus.

The mission of the La Salle University Art Museum is to further the University's Lasallian educational objectives by helping students, other members of the University community, and the general public to experience significant, original works of art in an intimate setting and to place them in meaningful contexts. In addition to acquiring, preserving, and exhibiting its collections, the museum offers viewers an opportunity to sharpen their aesthetic perception and to investigate the interrelationships that emerge between art and other disciplines. Following this mission, LSUAM is a "teaching museum" which collects, holds and interprets original artworks that serve as essential resources for educational instruction and research. LSUAM presents high-quality exhibitions, lectures and educational programs for the La Salle community as well as broader public audiences, including underserved preK-12 school groups and special needs groups. These activities support the University's Catholic Lasallian mission of experiential education, social justice, and service to the community. In the last fiscal year, total attendance was close to 12,000, including 2,500 La Salle students and over 5,000 local schoolchildren.

The Art Museum's comprehensive collection of European and American art currently features over 5,000 artworks, with examples of major artists and historical stylistic movements in a wide range of subjects and media. Highlights from the permanent collection include Jan Provost's *Nativity*, Tintoretto's *Portrait of an Unknown Gentleman*, Rembrandt Peale's *Self-Portrait*, Henry Ossawa Tanner's *Mary*, George Rouault's *Last Romantic*, Edouard Vuillard's *Madame Hessel in Conversation*, Dame Elizabeth Frink's *Walking Madonna*, and Alex Katz's *Portrait of Neil Welliver*. The collections have grown through purchases and gifts from Art Angel alumni and friends.

www.ingramcontent.com/pod-product-compliance
Lightning Source LLC
Chambersburg PA
CBHW050749180526
45159CB00003B/1402